A House Divided

Elijah and the Kings of Israel

John MacArthur

Thomas Nelson
Since 1798

NASHVILLE   DALLAS   MEXICO CITY   RIO DE JANEIRO

Published in Nashville, Tennessee, by Thomas Nelson. Thomas Nelson is a trademark of Thomas Nelson, Inc.

Published in association with the literary agency of Wolgemuth & Associates, Inc.

Layout, design, and writing assistance by Gregory C. Benoit Publishing, Old Mystic, CT. ⒼB

Thomas Nelson, Inc. titles may be purchased in bulk for educational, business, fund-raising, or sales promotional use. For information, please e-mail *SpecialMarkets@ThomasNelson.com*.

ISBN 978-1-4185-3691-6

Printed in the United States of America

09 10 11 12 13 WC 5 4 3 2 1

CONTENTS

The Divided Kingdom

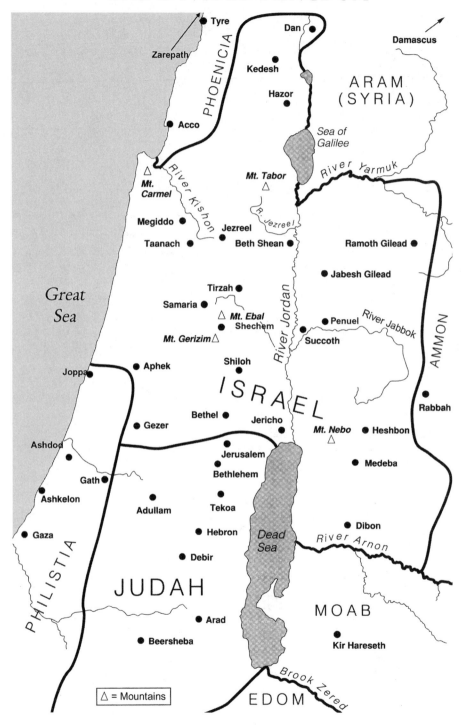

INTRODUCTION

When Israel entered the promised land they were a nation united, first under the leadership of judges and prophets, then under the leadership of kings. The Lord established the monarchies of Israel with the specific intention that the nation's kings should be shepherds of God's people. They were not to lord their power over the Israelites; instead the kings were to be examples of godliness and humility. Unfortunately, most of the nation's kings were unfaithful shepherds, and despite repeated prophetic confrontations, by and large the story of Israel's kings is the story of compromise and corruption—all at the expense of God's people.

These studies examine the lives of the kings of Israel, and you will have the opportunity to witness the ungodly decisions they made and what led them to make such bad choices. You will also meet those people who stood boldly against the idolatry and syncretism that polluted Israel, the prophets of God who proclaimed God's truth even at risk of their own lives.

In these twelve studies, we will jump back and forth in chronological history, looking at one historical period and then skipping forward or backward in time as needed. We will get to know Elijah and Obadiah, as well as Ahab and Jezebel. But through it all, we will learn some precious truths about the character of God, and we will see His great faithfulness in keeping His promises. We will learn, in short, what it means to walk by faith.

ᕬ WHAT WE'LL BE STUDYING ᕬ

This study guide is divided into four distinct sections in which we will examine selected Bible passages:

SECTION 1: HISTORY. In this first section, we will focus on the historical setting of our Bible text. These five lessons will give a broad overview of the people, places, and events that are important to this study. They will also provide the background for the next two sections. This is our most purely historical segment, focusing simply on what happened and why.

SECTION 2: CHARACTERS. The four lessons in this section will give us an opportunity to zoom in on the characters from our Scripture passages. Some of these people were introduced in section 1, but in this part of the study guide we will take a much closer look at these personalities. Why did God see fit to include them in His Book in the first place? What made them unique? What can we learn from their lives? In this practical section, we will answer all of these questions and more, as we learn how to live wisely by emulating the wisdom of those who came before us.

SECTION 3: THEMES. Section 3 consists of two lessons in which we will consider some of the broader themes and doctrines touched on in our selected Scripture passages. This is the guide's most abstract portion, wherein we will ponder specific doctrinal and theological questions that are important to the church today. As we ask what these truths mean to us as Christians, we will also look for practical ways to base our lives upon God's truth.

SECTION 4: SUMMARY AND REVIEW. In our final section, we will look back at the principles that we have discovered in the scriptures throughout this study guide. These will be our "takeaway" principles, those which permeate the Bible passages that we have studied. As always, we will be looking for ways to make these truths a part of our everyday lives.

✍ ABOUT THE LESSONS ✍

⇥ Each study begins with an introduction that provides the background for the selected Scripture passages.

⇥ To assist you in your reading, a section of notes—a miniature Bible commentary of sorts—offers both cultural information and additional insights.

⇥ A series of questions is provided to help you dig a bit deeper into the Bible text.

⇥ Overriding principles brought to light by the Bible text will be studied in each lesson. These principles summarize a variety of doctrines and practical truths found throughout the Bible.

⇥ Finally, additional questions will help you mine the deep riches of God's Word and, most importantly, to apply those truths to your own life.

Section 1:

History

In This Section:

— I —
GOD REJECTS SOLOMON

⌁ HISTORICAL BACKGROUND ⌁

Saul was chosen by God to become Israel's first king, but he did not walk in obedience to God's commands. The Lord eventually rejected him, and chose another to be king in his place. That man was David, whom the Lord declared to be a man after His own heart (1 Samuel 13:14; Acts 13:22). David did not live a sinless life; in fact, he committed both adultery and murder, bringing disaster upon his entire family and a civil war upon the nation of Israel. Yet his life overall was characterized by a steadfast desire to obey God's commands, and when he was confronted with his own sin, he repented immediately.

David's son Solomon succeeded him to the throne of Israel, and at first Solomon followed his father's example. The Lord appeared to him, offering him anything he asked for—and Solomon requested wisdom to rule God's people, rather than power or riches (1 Kings 3). The Lord was very pleased with the young king's request because it showed that he wanted to walk in the ways of God and be an example of godly leadership for His people.

Unfortunately, Solomon's wisdom did not restrain his flesh, and his reign quickly became marked by sin. He began by ignoring the Lord's injunction to remove the "high places," pagan shrines that were situated on hilltops and used by the Canaanites to worship false gods. This failure may have seemed fairly insignificant to Solomon at the time, but those high places would remain a stumbling block to Israel's future kings, as we will see in these studies. Solomon also had multiple wives, many of whom worshiped foreign gods. Those wives gradually led his heart away from the Lord, and he eventually joined them in their pagan practices in those very same high places that he had failed to eliminate.

As a result of his partial obedience, the Lord told Solomon that when he died, his son would see the kingdom divided into two separate nations. Only the tribe of Judah would remain loyal to Solomon, while the other ten tribes would become the nation of Israel. It is the kings of those ten tribes whom we will focus on in these studies. (For more on the kings of Judah, see the next book in this series, *Losing the Promised Land*.)

⚘ Reading 1 Kings 11:1–13 ⚘

A Divided Heart: *Solomon's reign may have begun well, but it did not finish well. He married hundreds of women, and they gradually led him away from God's commands.*

1. King Solomon loved many foreign women: Solomon was the wisest man in the world (1 Kings 3:12), yet he did not completely follow God's commands. He took many wives (see Deuteronomy 17:17) and he married foreign women (see Deuteronomy 7:1–4), both of which were contrary to God's will for His people. See the previous book in this series, *End of an Era*, for more information on Solomon.

4. his wives turned his heart after other gods: God had warned His people to not make marriages with those who didn't love Him. Likewise, today, the Bible warns Christians to not marry non-Christians, because such a marriage is like yoking two oxen together who want to go in different directions (2 Corinthians 6:14). A Christian who is unequally yoked in marriage to an unbeliever will face pressures to turn away from obedience to God's Word.

his heart was not loyal to the Lord his God: David, Solomon's father, did not live a life without sin. He, too, had several wives, and he committed adultery and then covertly arranged for the death of an innocent man, to cover his tracks. But the difference between King David and King Solomon was in their response to sin. When David was confronted by the prophet Nathan, he repented and turned away from his sinful behavior. His life was characterized by a determination to obey God's commandments, while Solomon's life was characterized by ongoing disobedience.

5. Ashtoreth . . . Milcom: Ashtoreth was the Canaanite goddess of love and fertility. Milcom was also called Molech, whose worship practices included child sacrifice. We will encounter these and other false deities throughout this study, as the subsequent kings of Israel repeatedly indulged in pagan practices.

6. did not fully follow the Lord: It is worth noting that Solomon did obey the Lord's commands on some levels in his life. For example, he built a temple to the Lord as commanded, and he wrote thousands of proverbs—many of which are included in the books of Proverbs and Ecclesiastes. Yet he also indulged in areas of direct disobedience to God's commands, and the Lord does not give His people the freedom to pick and choose which parts of His Word we will obey. This trend of partial obedience would plague the kingships of Israel for hundreds of years to come.

7. Solomon built a high place: A "high place" was a pagan shrine, generally located on a hilltop. Such shrines were very common when the Israelites entered the promised land, but the Lord had commanded them to destroy all sites of pagan worship (Deuteronomy 7:5). Rather than destroy them, however, the kings of Israel used them, and even created more of their own in pursuit of pagan idolatry. These high places will be mentioned frequently throughout these studies, since they played a large part in the sinful practices of Israel's kings.

Chemosh: A Moabite deity that required child sacrifice.

God Keeps His promise: *The Lord had promised Solomon that if he obeyed His commands, his throne would be established—and if he didn't, Israel would be torn apart.*

9. the Lord ... had appeared to him twice: God had appeared to Solomon in a dream (1 Kings 3:5) and offered him anything he wanted. Solomon asked for "an understanding heart," or wisdom, so he could rightly lead God's people. The Lord had been pleased by Solomon's request and had granted him great wisdom as well as wealth and power. God appeared to him a second time after Solomon had completed the temple (1 Kings 9:2), offering to establish Solomon's throne forever in Israel—if he continued to walk in obedience to God's commands. The Lord warned Solomon in the second vision, however, that He would cut off Israel if Solomon or his sons forsook the Lord and began pursuing false gods.

11. I will surely tear the kingdom away from you: Israel at this time was a united kingdom, twelve tribes unified under one king. As a result of Solomon's sins, however, the Lord determined to split the nation into two kingdoms, which became the nations of Israel and Judah.

12. for the sake of your father David: The Lord had made an unconditional covenant with David, establishing his throne forever (2 Samuel 7:12–16). It was through this covenant that God would eventually establish the reign of His Son, Jesus. The Lord had also promised David that He would not remove His mercy from his son, as He had from Saul, effectively promising that He would not expel Solomon from the throne. Nevertheless, Solomon's dynasty would end when he died.

13. I will give one tribe to your son: This was the tribe of Judah, which remained loyal to the descendants of David. (David was from the tribe of Judah.) This study will focus on the kings of Israel; for information on the kings of Judah, see the next study in this series, *Losing the Promised Land.*

Torn in Two: *The Lord fulfills His word to Solomon, raising up Jeroboam to split Israel into two separate nations. The tribe of Judah, however, will remain dedicated to the Davidic line and to Solomon's son.*

27. Solomon had built the Millo: King Solomon was renowned for his incredible building projects, one of which was the Millo. The Millo was a series of terraces that supported the hill above Jerusalem. Jeroboam was an overseer in some of these building projects, and therefore was himself a man of influence in the kingdom.

28. Jeroboam was a mighty man of valor: This phrase was used to describe some of the great warriors who fought under King David, Solomon's father. It is possible that Jeroboam had distinguished himself in battle, but it was his industrious character that led Solomon to place him in charge of his building projects.

The labor force of the house of Joseph: These were conscripted laborers, Israelites who served King Solomon in the arduous work of construction. In this position, Jeroboam would have been in close contact with many Israelites who were discontented with Solomon's leadership.

29. Ahijah the Shilonite: Ahijah was a prophet of the Lord who lived in Shiloh, about twenty miles north of Jerusalem. See the map in the Introduction.

31. ten tribes: These were the northern tribes, which retained the name of Israel.

32. one tribe: This was the tribe of Judah, which probably also included the tribe of Simeon (bringing the total to twelve, even though only eleven are mentioned here).

for the sake of My servant David: See note on verse 12, above.

34. I have made him ruler all the days of his life: The Lord had promised Solomon that He would not tear the kingdom away during his lifetime (v. 12).

because he kept My commandments and My statutes: David provides a stark contrast to the vast majority of Israel's kings, as we will see in these studies. He was a sinner like all other human beings, yet his heart was fixed on obeying the Lord's commands. His successors on Israel's throne, for the most part, showed contempt for God's Word by indulging in pagan practices.

36. My servant David: It is interesting that the Lord permitted Solomon's son to retain the kingship over one tribe, not for Solomon's sake but for David's sake. This was because He had promised David that one of his heirs would always occupy the throne in Israel (2 Samuel 7:16), and God always keeps His promises.

a lamp before Me: The lamp represented both the life of a person and his witness to God's faithfulness. As a lamp gives light in darkness, so God's people provide light to the world around them, showing forth the glory of God. The Lord intended that the entire nation of Israel, and her kings in particular, should be like lamps in the world, showing forth the grace and faithfulness of God. But Israel's kings consistently failed in this, leading the people of Israel away from God's commands. Ultimately, Jesus fulfilled this role, as both a descendant of David and the Light of the World (John 8:12).

37. KING OVER ISRAEL: That is, the ten northern tribes. Judah would remain under the authority of Solomon's son Rehoboam.

38. IF . . . THEN: God offered Jeroboam an enduring dynasty over the ten northern tribes of Israel, offering him the same promise that He had offered to David and Solomon (1 Kings 2:4; 3:14). But this was a conditional promise; Jeroboam needed to obey God's commands in order to receive God's promised blessing. If Jeroboam had been faithful to God, as David was, then his descendants would have inherited the throne of Israel, and his family's reign would have endured. He did not prove faithful, however, as we will see in Study 3.

39. BUT NOT FOREVER: David's descendants did not keep the Lord's commands, and therefore they were removed from the throne of Israel. But God made an unconditional promise to David that his offspring would rule over Israel forever, and that promise is ultimately fulfilled in Jesus, the Son of David.

↰ FIRST IMPRESSIONS ↱

1. *What does it mean that Solomon's heart was not loyal to God? How did this happen? How might it have been prevented?*

2. *Which of God's commands did Solomon keep? Which did he disobey?*

3. Why did God divide the kingdom of Israel into two separate nations? Why did He not simply remove the entire nation from Solomon's heirs?

4. In what ways was David different from Solomon? What does it mean to be "a man after God's own heart"?

⟿ Some Key Principles ⟿

God keeps His promises—both for blessing and for judgment.

The Lord had promised David that He would establish his throne and his kingdom forever (2 Samuel 7:12–16). He also promised David that He would embrace Solomon as His own son, disciplining him "with the rod of men and with the blows of the sons of men" (2 Samuel 7:14), yet further assuring that His mercy would never depart from David's son. The Lord kept this oath fully, both in the short term and the long term. In the short term, the Lord did chasten Solomon in order to lead him back into obedience to God's commands, and He did not remove Solomon from the throne as He had done to Saul. In the long term, the Lord fully established David's throne for all eternity through His Son, Jesus Christ.

The Lord had also made a similar promise to Solomon, that He would establish Solomon's throne and lineage for all time, as He had done for David—*if* Solomon would continue to walk in obedience to the Lord's commands (1 Kings 9:2–9). Notice that word *if* (v. 4). This promise was conditional; the Lord required Solomon's compliance with His will if he was to experience the blessings. The Lord also gave His word that if Solomon or his sons followed after false gods, then He would cut off Israel from the promised land. This promise, too, the Lord kept in full; when Solomon went in pursuit of foreign gods, the Lord split the nation in two.

The chief principle here is that God always keeps His word. This principle cuts both ways; the Lord keeps His promises of blessing for His people, and He also keeps His promises of discipline. In the long run, both sides of this are good news for God's people, since even His disciplines are intended for our good, not for our harm. God takes His vows very seriously, and so should His people.

Christians are called to complete obedience, not to partial obedience.

Solomon began his reign well, devoting himself to wisdom and to God's Word. But as time went along, he began to drift away from obedience, making compromises and choosing which of God's commands to obey and which to ignore. One of his first mistakes was to marry "foreign women," women whose hearts were devoted to foreign gods. This caused Solomon to be unequally yoked, and his many wives (another departure from God's commands) constantly urged him to join them in their pagan religious practices.

God does not give His people the option to customize His Word, choosing for themselves which principles they will incorporate into their lives and which commandments they will ignore. This would be like a soldier telling his commanding officer that he'll obey the officer's commands if and when he gets around to it. Yet this attitude is prevalent in God's church today, as believers attempt to rewrite Scripture to satisfy cultural norms or personal preferences.

The Lord expects His people to live in accordance with the full Word of God, following all of its precepts and living in obedience to all of its commandments. Solomon's life provides a sobering example of what can happen to Christians who pick and choose what parts of Scripture they will apply to their lives, and we will see this same trend in other kings of Israel. The Lord wants His people to take warning from the examples of these kings, devoting our hearts and minds to full obedience instead of following in their wayward footsteps.

We must guard our hearts against the seductions of the world.

We are told that Solomon's heart "was not loyal to the LORD his God" in his later years (1 Kings 11:4). This is a chilling statement, when we consider that Solomon was the wisest man who ever lived. How could the wisest man of all time allow his heart to grow cold to God—especially when he had begun his reign so well?

The fact is that the world around us has countless allurements and temptations, things that seem attractive on the surface but can eventually lead God's people away from Him into the pursuit of vain enticements. Even things that are good in themselves, such as work and home, can become so all-consuming that they gradually lure a person away from God.

The way to avoid this error is to continually be filling one's mind with the Word of God. Solomon himself wrote this advice: "My son, give attention to my words; incline your ear to my sayings. Do not let them depart from your eyes; keep them in the midst of your heart; for they are life to those who find them, and health to all their flesh. Keep your heart with all diligence, for out of it spring the issues of life" (Proverbs 4:20–23). Studying God's Word on a regular basis, along with obedience and prayer, enables us to be yielded to the Holy Spirit—and He will ensure that we are kept safe from the snares of the world (2 Thessalonians 3:3).

⌁ DIGGING DEEPER ⌁

5. In what ways did Solomon allow his heart to drift away from the Lord? What is required to prevent this?

6. What unconditional promises did God give to David and Solomon? What conditional promises did He make? Why does He sometimes put conditions on His blessings?

7. Which of God's promises bring you encouragement? Which provide a sober warning? When have you seen His promises come true in your own life?

8. What does it mean to guard your heart? How is this done, in practical terms?

⌒ TAKING IT PERSONALLY ⌒

9. Are there areas of God's Word that you are choosing to disregard in your life? What is necessary for you to fully obey Scripture?

10. What forces of the world are trying to divide your heart, pulling you away from God? How can you strengthen your undivided loyalty to Him?

2

ISRAEL SPLITS IN TWO

ᔆ HISTORICAL BACKGROUND ᔆ

Solomon, the wisest man who ever lived, ruled as Israel's king for forty years. At the time of his death, all twelve tribes of Israel functioned together as one nation, but this situation was soon to change.

When Solomon died, his son Rehoboam took the throne as king of the united tribes of Israel. The people of Israel had suffered under the heavy hand of Solomon's taxation and conscripted labor, and the change of kingship gave them hope for some relief. As they approached their new king with this hope, they requested that he ease their taxes and remove the burden of forced labor from their shoulders.

Rehoboam was forty-one years old when he took the throne, and the men who had advised his father were considerably older. But Rehoboam also brought along his own counselors, men who had grown up with him and had been his personal friends for many years. These men had probably been raised under privileged circumstances, enjoying the powers and privileges of royal favor all their lives. Like Rehoboam, they had no firsthand experience in the affairs of governing Israel, and lacked the wisdom of the elders who had advised Solomon.

The young king turns to his counselors for advice concerning the people's complaint, which is a wise thing for any ruler to do. Unfortunately, Rehoboam's young friends prove to be unwise advisers, and Rehoboam becomes an equally unwise king.

ᔆ READING 1 KINGS 12:1–24 ᔆ

THE PEOPLE'S COMPLAINT: *Rehoboam, Solomon's son, becomes king after his father's death. The people of Israel come to him with a request, and he is faced with a decision.*

1. REHOBOAM: Solomon's son.

SHECHEM: Approximately thirty miles north of Jerusalem. See the map in the Introduction.

4. YOUR FATHER MADE OUR YOKE HEAVY: Solomon had instituted a conscripted labor force in Israel in order to build his great projects (1 Kings 5:13), and he had also inflicted heavy taxes on the people in order to pay for those projects (1 Kings 4:7, 27–28). This apparently was the central issue on the minds of the people, much as the economy and taxes figure prominently in people's politics today, and they were willing to follow Solomon's son if he simply lessened these burdens. But the Lord's concerns were not with Israel's financial economy, but with the spiritual condition of her leaders.

6. THE ELDERS: Solomon's counselors and cabinet ministers. These men would probably have been a good deal older than Rehoboam, since they had served when his father was king.

7. IF YOU WILL BE A SERVANT TO THESE PEOPLE: The elders gave Rehoboam very good counsel. A wise king will be a servant to his people, a principle which the Lord of Creation demonstrated when He washed His disciples' feet (John 13:3–17). The people's request was not excessive, and Rehoboam could have granted it without much sacrifice.

8. THE YOUNG MEN WHO HAD GROWN UP WITH HIM: Rehoboam was in his early forties when he became king, and these counselors were in his own age range. He had evidently surrounded himself with his friends, perhaps creating offices for them to fill. It was wise of Rehoboam to seek counsel before making a decision, but it would have been far wiser to listen to the advice of those who were older and more experienced in the court of Solomon.

10. THICKER THAN MY FATHER'S WAIST: This was a proverb of the time, meaning that Rehoboam's most lenient measures would be more severe and powerful than Solomon's strongest measures.

11. WHIPS . . . SCOURGES: A whip is a single cord of leather, but a scourge had many cords attached—often with bits of bone or sharp stone at the ends to tear the flesh. Rehoboam's burden on the people would be far more severe and cutting than what they had experienced under his father, Solomon. Rehoboam's attitude toward his power was despotic, and not in keeping with the specific model that the Lord had given concerning His chosen king (Deuteronomy 17:14–20).

THE PEOPLE REBEL: *Rehoboam's response turns the people of Israel against him, and the kingdom splits into two nations.*

15. THE TURN OF EVENTS WAS FROM THE LORD: From a human perspective, Rehoboam might have prevented the national division simply by listening to the people and to the wise advice of his elders. But God had already determined that it should take place so "that He might fulfill His word." God sovereignly used the foolishness of Rehoboam to fulfill Ahijah's prophecy (1 Kings 11:29–39).

16. WHAT SHARE HAVE WE IN DAVID? : A man named Sheba had once rebelled against King David using almost identical words as his rallying cry ("We have no share in David" [2 Samuel 20:1]). The people of Israel were openly rejecting David and his descendants as their rightful king. Bear in mind, however, that these were the people of the ten northern tribes of Israel; the people of Judah remained loyal to the house of David, and accepted Rehoboam as their king.

18. ADORAM: Adoram, also called Adoniram, had been the overseer for forced labor and taxation throughout Israel, under both David (2 Samuel 20:24) and Solomon (1 Kings 4:6). From a human viewpoint, it was probably a very foolish tactic to send the overseer of forced labor to negotiate with the men of Israel at this point, but we must remember that the Lord is in control of all events, and He was guiding these events intentionally to lead to the split in the kingdom.

ALL ISRAEL STONED HIM WITH STONES: Killing such a high court official was an act of open revolution against the king. The men who committed this act presumably would not hesitate to murder Rehoboam himself as well. The men of Israel were not justified in committing this crime, even though it was part of God's plan to divide the kingdom. They were still fully accountable before the Lord for this act of murder.

19. ISRAEL HAS BEEN IN REBELLION: God's Word teaches us that rebellion is the same as the sin of witchcraft (1 Samuel 15:23). We must recognize that the Lord was bringing about the fulfillment of His determination to split the nation, but He still was not pleased by the sinful actions of His people. God may choose to use the wicked deeds of men to accomplish His purposes, but that does not exonerate those who commit the deeds.

20. MADE HIM KING OVER ALL ISRAEL: It is interesting that the people of Israel (the ten northern tribes) evidently anointed Jeroboam as king without involving the priests. Up to this point, the Lord had anointed each king of Israel through His priests, indicating that the king had been chosen by God. In this case, the king of the northern tribes had been chosen by the people. There is no indication that the people even consulted the Lord on the matter.

24. THIS THING IS FROM ME: That is, the Lord had decreed that the nation of Israel would be split in two. The method of rebellion and the murderous deeds of individuals, however, were not countenanced by God.

ꙮ First Impressions ꙮ

1. *If you had been in Rehoboam's position, how might you have responded to the Israelites' complaints? Whose counsel would you have followed?*

2. *In what sense would Rehoboam have been a servant to the people if he had granted their requests? What role was he taking on when he refused to grant them?*

3. *In your opinion, what reasons might Rehoboam have had in setting up friends of his own age as his counselors? Why did he also retain the elders?*

4. *Why did the people of Israel murder Adoram? Why did they reject Rehoboam? What should their response have been?*

↶ Some Key Principles ↷

The Lord calls us to serve one another.

Rehoboam's counselors advised him to "be a servant to these people today, and serve them, and answer them, and speak good words to them" (1 Kings 12:7). Their counsel was very wise, and Rehoboam should have heeded it. While the Scriptures show that humility makes a person's life receptive to grace, the world would have us believe that humility is a sign of inferiority. This evidently was Rehoboam's mistaken mind-set, as he strove to demonstrate his power and majesty by threatening to be even harsher and more demanding than his father had been.

Jesus provides us with the opposite example. He is the King of kings and Lord of lords, more powerful and majestic than the greatest kings who ever lived—and yet He bowed Himself before His own servants and humbly washed their feet. The Lord also commanded His disciples to follow His example, being willing to serve one another even in such lowly occupations as washing one another's feet.

Servanthood is neither an option nor something that some are "called to" and others are not—it is a command that the Lord gives to all of His followers. If we want to follow Him, we must obey Him, and part of that obedience includes being a willing servant to others. "If I then, your Lord and Teacher, have washed your feet, you also ought to wash one another's feet. For I have given you an example, that you should do as I have done to you" (John 13:14–15).

Rebellion is like the sin of witchcraft.

The people of Israel rebelled against Rehoboam, even though he was chosen of God to be Solomon's successor to the throne. It is true that the Lord used this rebellion to accomplish His own purposes, but we must not lose sight of the fact that the people's rebellion was sinful in God's eyes.

The Lord declared that "rebellion is as the sin of witchcraft, and stubbornness is as iniquity and idolatry" (1 Samuel 15:23). Lucifer committed rebellion against God, and raised himself up to be equal with God (Isaiah 14:12–15), and those who rebel against God's chosen authority effectively follow in the devil's footsteps. When we rebel against the Lord, we are removing Him from authority in our lives and setting ourselves in His place. This is essentially what the people of Israel did when they threw down Rehoboam and set up the man of their own choosing.

As Christians, we are to submit ourselves both to the Lord and to those whom He has placed in authority over us. Jesus, the Lord of the universe, voluntarily submitted Himself to the religious and political authorities of His day—even to the point of allowing them to crucify Him. "Therefore," Peter wrote, "submit yourselves to every ordinance of man for the Lord's sake, whether to the king as supreme, or to governors, as to those who are sent by him for the punishment of evildoers and for the praise of those who do good" (1 Peter 2:13–14).

Divine sovereignty does not nullify human responsibility.

The Lord prophesied that He would tear the kingdom away from Solomon's son, dividing the nation of Israel into two separate kingdoms. He brought this about, using the foolish decisions of Rehoboam and the rebellious spirit of Israel to accomplish His purpose—yet this did not exonerate the king of Israel from culpability for his foolishness, while the people of Israel were also responsible for their sin. God is indeed sovereign over all the affairs of mankind, but this does not mean that He will not judge individuals for their actions.

Jesus again provides the perfect example of this principle. It was God's plan from the foundation of the world that His perfect Son should offer Himself as a sacrifice to redeem sinful men, and God used the evil deeds of those who rejected Christ to accomplish that plan. Yet this did not exonerate those who crucified Christ; neither does it exonerate anyone who rejects Jesus as the only way to salvation and peace with God.

The good news in this principle is that God uses all things to further His purposes in our lives. When we live in obedience to His Word, we can rest in the assurance that God is completely sovereign over all the events and circumstances that come our way, and He will turn all things to His glory and our blessing. "All things work together for good to those who love God, to those who are the called according to His purpose" (Romans 8:28).

Digging Deeper

5. *Why did God permit the people to commit rebellion and murder? Why does His sovereign use of such deeds not exonerate people from personal responsibility?*

6. What reasons might Rehoboam have had for answering the people in such harsh terms? What might he have hoped to accomplish? What was wrong with his thinking?

7. Why did God choose to split the kingdom in two? At what points might He have chosen to not do so? What human actions moved Him in this direction?

8. Why does God say that rebellion is like the sin of witchcraft? How are the two sins related? What does this suggest about the seriousness of a rebellious spirit?

Taking It Personally

9. *Do you generally prefer to serve or to be served? Which role tends to characterize your life more? What areas of service might the Lord be calling you to?*

10. *How do you generally respond to authority? Are there areas of rebellion in your life? What needs to change in your thinking or your actions?*

THE KINGS OF ISRAEL*

Ruler	Reign (BC)**	Length (years)
Saul	1050–1010	40
David	1010–970	40
Solomon	970–930	40
Jeroboam I	930–910	22
Nadab	910–909	2
Baasha	909–886	24
Elah	886–885	2
Zimri	885	(7 days)
Omri	885–874	12
Ahab	874–853	22
Ahaziah	853–852	2
Joram (Jehoram)	852–841	12
Jehu	841–814	28
Jehoahaz	814–798	17
Jehoash (Joash)	798–882	16
Jeroboam II	782 (793)–753	41
Zechariah	753–752	(6 months)
Shallum	752	(1 month)
Menahem	752–742	10
Pekahiah	742–740	2
Pekah	740 (752)–732	20
Hoshea	732–722	9
10 northern tribes enter captivity	722	

* For the kings of Judah, see the next book in this series, *Losing the Promised Land*.

** Dates are approximate. (Dates in parentheses indicate a co-regency of father and son.)

— 3 —
ISRAEL'S CHOSEN KING

↳ HISTORICAL BACKGROUND ↰

As we saw in our last study, the people of Israel rejected Rehoboam, Solomon's son, as their king when he treated them disgracefully. In his place, they elevated Jeroboam to the throne and swore their allegiance to him. These things, of course, did not catch the Lord by surprise; this was all part of His plan for the nation of Israel. The Lord had even promised Jeroboam that his authority would be secure and his sons would follow him on the throne—if he only walked in obedience to God's commands.

So Jeroboam had nothing to fear as he took command. All that was required of him was to obey God's Word, and he was assured of blessing and success. But Jeroboam did not see things that way. He convinced himself that the people of Israel would turn against him once they got a chance, changing their minds and returning to Rehoboam—and killing him in the process. These fears were groundless; there was no indication, as far as we are told, that the people even entertained such thoughts. Essentially, he was doubting the Word of God.

Fear is often like that: it ignores facts and logic, and takes control of our hearts and minds—if we allow it to. Jeroboam allowed his fears to guide him, and as a result he walked into grievous sin instead of walking in God's promises. What's worse, he led the entire nation of Israel into idolatry, all because he did not trust in the Lord's faithfulness.

↳ READING 1 KINGS 12:25–13:10 ↰

KING JEROBOAM BECOMES AFRAID: *Jeroboam persuades himself that the Israelites will turn against him if they travel to Jerusalem, so he concocts a wicked scheme.*

12:25. SHECHEM ... PENUEL: Jeroboam fortified the city of Shechem, located in the hill country north of Jerusalem. Penuel was directly west, situated on the River Jabbok. Jeroboam apparently intended to establish his authority over the people of Israel on both sides of the Jordan River. See the map in the Introduction for the locations of these cities.

26. Jeroboam said in his heart: The Lord had offered Jeroboam complete security for his throne and for his posterity, if he would only obey God's commands and follow in His ways (1 Kings 11:38). But Jeroboam's heart was not turned toward God, and he did not place his trust in the Lord's faithfulness. He allowed his own fears to lead him into sin, fears that the people of Israel would change their minds and make Solomon's son Rehoboam their king.

27. the house of the Lord at Jerusalem: The Lord had directed Solomon to construct a permanent temple in Jerusalem to become the site of worship for the entire nation of Israel. The ark of the covenant, which represented God's presence with His people, was there, and all Israelites were to offer their sacrifices at that location. Jeroboam's lack of trust in God's truthfulness actually led him to assume that, if the people walked in obedience to His commands, then they would remove him from the throne—even though the Lord had placed him there in the first place. This cockeyed reasoning motivated him to lead the people away from obedience and into idolatry.

28. two calves of gold: Aaron had set up a golden calf during Israel's exodus from Egypt, and the Lord's wrath had burned fiercely when the people bowed in worship before it. Jeroboam presented his golden calves to the people using almost the very same words that Aaron had used (Exodus 32:4).

A More Comfortable Religion: *Jeroboam seduces the people of Israel to join him in idolatry by offering them an easier, less costly way of worship.*

It is too much for you: Jeroboam presented three arguments in support of his idolatrous plan: (1) worshiping the Lord in Jerusalem is inconvenient, and the calves will make worship less burdensome; (2) the calves are actually gods, containing some mystical power to protect and forgive the people; (3) our ancestors did it, so it must be right. These three lies are still prevalent in the world today, and even Christians can fall prey to them. The church, too, often disregards Scripture's teachings in favor of that which seems expedient, less inconvenient, or more "relevant." The world claims that every religious system has something to offer, and we are pressured to place our faith in just about anything but the Word of God. But false religions have been around for a very long time, as have the lies of the evil one, and the antiquity of a belief system does not mean that it is true.

29. Bethel ... Dan: Jeroboam went out of his way to make his false religion as convenient as possible. Bethel was located near the southern border of his kingdom, while Dan was up near the northern border. (See the map in the Introduction.) The country was now bracketed by cow worship, rather than God worship.

30. THIS THING BECAME A SIN: That is, Jeroboam's actions led the entire nation of Israel into sin. It is unquestionably a sin to set up golden calves and tell others that they are gods, but Jeroboam's position as king gave his lies greater authority, causing his sin to spread throughout the land.

31. SHRINES ON THE HIGH PLACES: The high places, as we have seen in a previous study, were hilltop sanctuaries used by the Canaanites for their pagan worship practices. The Lord had forbidden His people to use pagan sites for their worship (Numbers 33:52), and His people were to worship Him only at the temple once Solomon had constructed it. But Solomon himself had ignored this command, and now we begin to see its fruit being borne under his successors. These high places will continue to plague the nation of Israel throughout our studies.

INVENTING A NEW RELIGION: *The king next appoints his own priesthood for his new religion, and even invents a special holiday—to coincide with God's chosen feast.*

PRIESTS FROM EVERY CLASS OF PEOPLE: Here we discover another crafty technique that Jeroboam used in selling his false religion: he removed "class boundaries," making the priesthood available to everyone. The Lord, however, had expressly chosen only the men who were descended from Aaron as His priests, who were members of the tribe of Levi (Numbers 3:10). This move on Jeroboam's part was another act of expediency, since his false religion could call upon people who lived near his many shrines, rather than strictly Levites, to act as priests.

32. JEROBOAM ORDAINED A FEAST: The Feast of Tabernacles would have occurred around the same time in Jerusalem, and Jeroboam was deliberately trying to compete with God's ordained time of worship. In so doing, he was actually raising himself far above his proper kingly authority, to the point that he was even ordaining religious festivals as though he were in the place of God.

OFFERED SACRIFICES ON THE ALTAR: Jeroboam also took upon himself the role of a priest, just as Saul had done several generations earlier (1 Samuel 13). The Lord had rejected Saul for his sinful presumption, yet Jeroboam's act is even more depraved, since he was acting as a priest before the idols he had created.

CONFRONTED BY A PROPHET: *The Lord sends a man of God to confront the king, and prophesies that God's judgment would fall upon his apostasy.*

13:1. FROM JUDAH: The Lord sent a prophet from the nation loyal to David's line to rebuke the now idolatrous north. This would add extra insult to the rebuke the prophet was about to bring.

2. JOSIAH: Josiah would become king in Judah some three hundred years after this prophecy, and he did destroy the altar and even burned the bones of the very priests whom Jeroboam had appointed. See 2 Kings 22–23 for the full account.

4. HIS HAND . . . WITHERED: The Lord miraculously intervened as Jeroboam tried to arrest the man of God, removing the vitality from the very hand that was reaching out against God's prophet. This dramatic sign also demonstrated that Jeroboam's kingly power would wither up as well.

5. THE ALTAR ALSO WAS SPLIT APART: The torn altar was a clear visible demonstration of the way God destroys all false idols. The ashes spilling on the ground indicated that even the offerings and sacrifices that had been made on that altar were contemptible, deserving to be trampled underfoot by men and animals alike.

6. PRAY FOR ME: Roles were reversed between the mighty king and the lowly prophet when the king stretched out his hand and asked for healing. Jeroboam would have been unlikely to show any mercy to the prophet, but in contrast the Lord demonstrated His great mercy by restoring the king's hand to its former health. Strangely enough, despite the miraculous events Jeroboam had seen, he refused to repent.

8. I WOULD NOT GO IN WITH YOU: Jeroboam made a great show of offering reward and fellowship to the man of God, perhaps in order to show the people of Israel that he had God's blessing once again. But sharing a meal with another man in that day indicated intimate fellowship, and the prophet refused to dine with the king because the Lord would have no communion with Jeroboam's false gods.

ᕗ First Impressions ᕗ

1.   *Why did Jeroboam create the golden calves? What motivated him to do such a thing?*

2. *What tactics did Jeroboam use to seduce the people of Israel into worshiping his calves? How does the world today apply similar pressures to God's people?*

3. *Why did the man of God refuse the king's gifts? Why did he decline to eat with the king? What does this show about God's attitude toward idolatry?*

4. *Why did Jeroboam create a new class of priests? Why did he create a new holiday? How do we see similar tendencies in the church today?*

↝ Some Key Principles ↜

Fear often comes from doubts about God.

Jeroboam convinced himself through fear that the people of Israel would turn against him once they began traveling to Jerusalem to worship; he feared for his throne, his kingdom, his very life. This fear led him to take rash steps in self-defense—even though nobody had even threatened him. He set up false idols and invented a whole new religion, just out of fear that the Israelites would turn against him if they worshiped God in Jerusalem, as He had commanded them to do.

The reality is that God had solemnly promised Jeroboam that his throne would be secure, both for himself and for his descendants, if he would just walk in compliance with His stated will. He had nothing to fear whatsoever; even if some people had decided in the future to turn against his authority, the Lord would have preserved him just as He did for David.

Fear causes us to move away from the Lord, not toward Him. Anxiety and worry are symptoms of a lack of trust in God's faithfulness, because God always keeps His promises. The antidote to fear is to meditate upon God's promises, and remind ourselves from Scripture that He is always faithful. If Jeroboam had believed God's promises, he would have avoided grievous sin—and he would have not led the entire nation of Israel into apostasy.

Christians must honor the Lord's commands concerning spiritual headship.

There is a certain irony in Jeroboam's decision to create a new priesthood in Israel. He was afraid that the people would rebel against his authority, even though that authority had been appointed by God, and he dealt with that imagined threat by rebelling against God's chosen priestly authority.

The Lord had commanded that only men from the tribe of Levi could become priests, but that didn't fit in with Jeroboam's plan to keep the people of Israel away from Jerusalem. So he ignored that stipulation and appointed his own priesthood from every class of people within Israel, people undoubtedly selected for their willingness to disregard God's commands. In the minds of such people, the Lord's stipulations for spiritual authority had ceased to be relevant, and it was perfectly acceptable to rewrite those laws.

The church today faces the same pressures in this regard. God's Word is clear on the subject of having qualified leadership within the local church and male headship within the home, but the world pressures Christians to disregard those directions as being outdated and no longer relevant in the twenty-first century. God's people must not be led away from His Word, however; the Lord wants men to rise up and take the lead in their churches and their homes, regardless of what the world around us thinks.

Stand guard against idolatry.

King Jeroboam became fearful that the people of Israel would abandon him as their leader if they traveled to Jerusalem to worship the Lord, so he decided to create some idols for the people to worship instead. He went well beyond this, in fact, by creating an entire religious system around his golden calves—appointing priests, establishing several centers of worship, even creating a special feast day for his newly invented religion.

Jeroboam clearly committed idolatry when he constructed two golden calves and set them up for public adoration. Yet his idolatry was even craftier and subtler than that, and his actions illustrate the ways in which the world pressures Christians to create their own golden calves. Our own interests can become idols in our lives, motivating us to depart from obedience to God's Word, even as Jeroboam did out of concern for his own kingship.

Career goals, financial aspirations, dreams of the future, worldly prestige, and many other concerns can creep into our hearts like an insidious vine, choking out our commitment to the Lord. It is even possible to allow something that is legitimate and good in its own right to become so important in our hearts that it becomes an idol. Anything that takes priority over God's Word has become a golden calf in our lives. "You shall have no other gods before Me. . . . For I, the LORD your God, am a jealous God" (Exodus 20:3, 5).

↳ DIGGING DEEPER ↰

5. *Why did Jeroboam fall into fear? How did the fear influence his judgment? How might he have avoided this whole situation?*

6. In what ways did Solomon's actions have an influence in Jeroboam's day? How might things have been different if Solomon had destroyed the high places?

7. What idols do people worship in the modern world? When have you struggled with something that was becoming an idol in your life?

8. What does Scripture teach about a man's responsibilities in the home? in the church? How do these teachings compare with the world's beliefs?

ᔕ Taking It Personally ᔕ

9. Are there any idols in your life? What things threaten to compete with your devotion to the Lord? How can you remove these threats?

10. Do you tend to be fearful or anxious? What causes your worries? What promises of God can you apply to those things?

THE MINISTRY OF ELIJAH

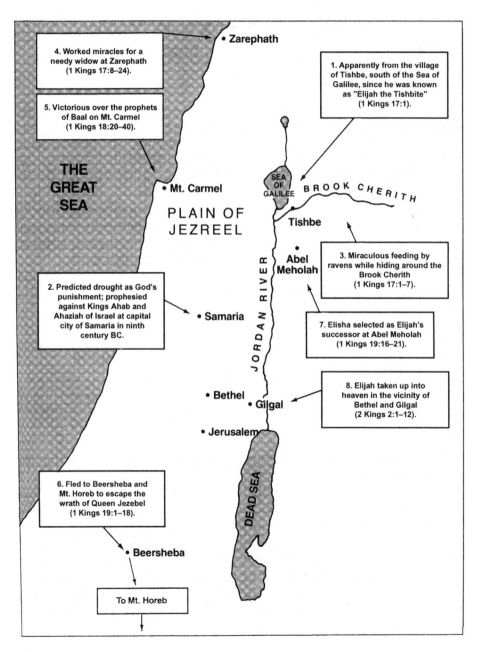

4. Worked miracles for a needy widow at Zarephath (1 Kings 17:8–24).

5. Victorious over the prophets of Baal on Mt. Carmel (1 Kings 18:20–40).

1. Apparently from the village of Tishbe, south of the Sea of Galilee, since he was known as "Elijah the Tishbite" (1 Kings 17:1).

• Zarephath

THE GREAT SEA

• Mt. Carmel

PLAIN OF JEZREEL

SEA OF GALILEE

BROOK CHERITH

Tishbe

• Abel Meholah

3. Miraculous feeding by ravens while hiding around the Brook Cherith (1 Kings 17:1–7).

2. Predicted drought as God's punishment; prophesied against Kings Ahab and Ahaziah of Israel at capital city of Samaria in ninth century BC.

• Samaria

JORDAN RIVER

7. Elisha selected as Elijah's successor at Abel Meholah (1 Kings 19:16–21).

• Bethel

• Gilgal

8. Elijah taken up into heaven in the vicinity of Bethel and Gilgal (2 Kings 2:1–12).

• Jerusalem

6. Fled to Beersheba and Mt. Horeb to escape the wrath of Queen Jezebel (1 Kings 19:1–18).

DEAD SEA

• Beersheba

To Mt. Horeb

∼ 4 ∼
THE KINGSHIP OF AHAB

∼ HISTORICAL BACKGROUND ∼

After Jeroboam, Israel had five different kings in quick succession, and each of them did evil in the sight of the Lord. Most followed Jeroboam's example by attempting to mix the worship of pagan gods with the worship of the Lord. This parade of wicked kings turned Israel into a pagan nation, one where the worship of the true God was almost unheard of. But despite the wickedness of these kings, the worst for Israel was still ahead.

King Ahab came to power fifty years after Jeroboam had died, and he would give Israel a new standard for wickedness. Ahab's father, King Omri, had purchased a hill northwest of Shechem and had built a fortified city there named Samaria. Ahab made this his capital city, and he added a temple to it. That temple, however, was dedicated not to the worship of the Lord but to a heathen god. Israel's Canaanite neighbors worshiped a false god named Baal, whom they believed was responsible for sending rain and fruitful harvests. Ahab turned his heart fully to Baal worship, and he led the entire nation into pagan practices.

Ahab's wife was a woman named Jezebel, a name that has become synonymous with treachery. She was the daughter of a Canaanite king, and was also a priestess to Baal. It is not surprising that Ahab followed her lead, for we will see in future studies that she was a woman who knew how to take charge and get things done.

The things that got done during Ahab's reign, however, were exceedingly wicked—yet even in the midst of such wickedness, the Lord sent His people a prophet, giving them another chance to turn back to Him.

∼ READING 1 KINGS 16:29–17:9 ∼

AHAB AND JEZEBEL: *The royal crown has been passed six times since Jeroboam's rule, each new king doing evil in the sight of the Lord. But Ahab and Jezebel will outdo them all.*

16:29. AHAB: There were five kings between Jeroboam and Ahab, including Omri, Ahab's father. Ahab, however, proved to be one of the wickedest kings in Israel's history. (See the full list of Israel's kings on page 24.)

SAMARIA: Ahab's father, Omri, had built a city on the hill, which he called Samaria, seven miles northwest of Shechem. (See the map in the Introduction.) Its central location was very convenient for everyone in Israel, and the city became Israel's equivalent of Jerusalem. Its people became known as *Samaritans*, and they figure in many Gospel passages of the New Testament.

30. AHAB . . . DID EVIL IN THE SIGHT OF THE LORD: This somber statement summarizes each of the preceding kings, as well, all the way back to Jeroboam. But Ahab would outdo them all. In fact, the verse goes on to say that he did "more [evil] than all who were before him."

31. AS THOUGH IT HAD BEEN A TRIVIAL THING: Jeroboam had established a precedent for the kings of Israel when he instituted idolatry, and his successors followed in his footsteps. But Ahab considered those sins to be normal for Israel's kings, and that attitude led him even deeper into sin.

JEZEBEL: This wicked woman became the very picture of treachery and guile. Her father was both king and high priest of Tyre and Sidon, and she was a priestess of Baal. She exercised profound influence over her husband, inciting him to great evil against the prophets of God, as we will see in a future study.

OFFICIAL STATE RELIGION: *Ahab takes Jeroboam's idolatry to its logical conclusion. Where Jeroboam mixed true worship with paganism, Ahab embraces pure pagan idolatry.*

BAAL: The predominant god in Canaanite religion. The pagans worshipped him as the one who sent rain and provided abundant crops. While Jeroboam had combined paganism with the worship of God, Ahab forsook Israel's God altogether and followed his wife into Baal worship.

32. TEMPLE OF BAAL: Jeroboam opened the door for Israel to stop worshiping God in Jerusalem, and Ahab went further by establishing a national temple to Baal in Samaria. This temple, with its altar and wooden image (v. 33), promoted Baal worship to the official state religion in Israel. What Jeroboam began, Ahab completed.

33. PROVOKE THE LORD GOD OF ISRAEL TO ANGER: Ahab and Jezebel led the nation of Israel to reject God as their Lord, a sin which Elijah combated during his ministry. In the end, however, Ahab's wickedness paved the way for the final collapse of Israel.

34. HIEL OF BETHEL BUILT JERICHO: The Lord had destroyed Jericho centuries earlier when Joshua led the people of Israel into the promised land. The Lord had forbidden the city's rebuilding, but also prophesied that one day a man would do so at the cost of two sons' lives (Joshua 6:26). It is no coincidence that the people of Israel would disregard such a dire warning from the Lord during the days of Ahab's reign; they were already treating His Word with contempt.

ENTER ELIJAH: *In the midst of Israel's wickedness, the Lord shows His mercy by sending His prophet to turn the nation's heart back to Himself.*

17:1. ELIJAH: The prophet's name means "the Lord is God," and Elijah's ministry consisted of urging the people of Israel to recognize God as their Lord. He was from a town named Tishbe, located east of the Jordan near the River Jabbok.

BEFORE WHOM I STAND: Elijah took a firm and public stand for God, right from the beginning of his ministry. He then called upon the people of Israel to join him, making up their minds whom to serve. This is a demonstration of God's great mercy to the people of Israel that He would send His prophet to call the people to repentance even in the midst of Ahab's determined wickedness. Elijah was also extremely bold in approaching the king, always without an invitation and generally without a welcome, but it was as nothing to speak to an earthly king when one stood in the presence of almighty God.

DEW NOR RAIN: The Lord had warned Israel that He would withhold water from them if they went in pursuit of foreign gods (Deuteronomy 11:16–17). Yet a drought was also a suitable punishment upon those people who ascribed the spring rains to a false deity. The drought lasted three and a half years (James 5:17).

3. HIDE BY THE BROOK CHERITH: Ahab proved hostile to Elijah's bold pronouncements, so the Lord withdrew His chosen prophet from His people for a season, allowing them to discover what life would be like if they continued to reject Him. The location of the brook is not known, but it might have been a seasonal brook that flowed during the rainy season and dried up at other times.

4. I HAVE COMMANDED THE RAVENS: While Ahab was leading Israel to believe that a nonexistent entity called Baal had control over the earth and its forces, the Lord of Creation was reminding Elijah that it is *He* who commands the natural world.

5. HE WENT AND DID ACCORDING TO THE WORD OF THE LORD: This statement characterized Elijah's life, as we will see in future studies. But his immediate obedience also stood as a condemnation against the kings of Israel, who stubbornly refused to obey God's commands.

Miraculous Provision: *The Lord provides for Elijah's physical needs, just as He did for Israel during the exodus.*

6. The ravens brought him bread and meat: The Lord had provided food and water miraculously for the Israelites during their exodus from Egypt, raining down manna and pouring water from rocks, prior to entering the promised land by crossing the Jordan River. It was a tragic irony here, however, that the prophet of God was banished to the other side of the Jordan, where he was miraculously provided with food and water while the people of Israel endured a terrible drought.

7. the brook dried up: The Lord is not limited in the methods He uses to accomplish His purposes, and He may choose to "dry up" a source of provision for His people. When He does, however, it is because He intends to provide for His people through another source. Elijah had depending not on the brook but on the God who created the brook. Even though the brook dried up, Elijah knew that his God would continue to provide.

8. Then the word of the Lord came to him: Notice that the Lord sent word to Elijah after the brook had dried up, not before. He sometimes calls His servants to trust Him through times of uncertainty or hardship.

9. go to Zarephath: This was a city located between Tyre and Sidon—the territory ruled over by Jezebel's father! Thus God sent His servant into the very heart of Baal worship, providing for him miraculously in the midst of drought and famine. In so doing, the Lord also provided a testimony to the heathen nations, demonstrating that the true God of Israel was also Lord of all creation.

a widow: We will meet this widow in Study 9.

⤳ First Impressions ⤶

1. *What might have motivated Ahab to become a Baal worshiper? What role might politics have played? What role might Jezebel have played?*

2. Why did Ahab view the sins of Jeroboam as though they were trivial things (16:31)? How did this attitude affect his decisions? His influence as king?

3. Why did Ahab build a temple to Baal in Samaria? How would this have affected him politically? How would it have affected the people of Israel?

4. Why did God send a drought on Israel? Why did He make special provision for Elijah? Why was Elijah given authority to end the drought?

⤙ Some Key Principles ⤚

Sin is never trivial.

Jeroboam instituted idolatry in Israel, attempting to mix it together with the nation's worship of God. This was a grievous sin, for which Jeroboam was judged by the Lord, yet Ahab acted "as though it had been a trivial thing" (1 Kings 16:31). By the time Ahab became king, the nation had been embracing Jeroboam's sinful practices for some fifty years, and the people had probably grown so accustomed to it that it seemed normal. This attitude of shrugging off sin led Ahab into even greater wickedness, and eventually brought about the downfall of all Israel.

Sin is never trivial in God's eyes, but when it is ignored or indulged, a believer can become inured. We can grow so accustomed to wickedness that we cease to be bothered by it, even accepting it as normal behavior in the world around us. The danger of this nonchalance is that if we don't take sin seriously, we can begin to slide into embracing it ourselves.

God hates sin, and He calls His people to hate it as He does. It is easy to become complacent about disobedience, and believers must guard against becoming comfortable with sin by spending time in God's Word and in regular fellowship with other believers. As James warns us, "Friendship with the world is enmity with God[.] Whoever therefore wants to be a friend of the world makes himself an enemy of God. . . . Draw near to God and He will draw near to you. Cleanse your hands, you sinners; and purify your hearts, you double-minded" (James 4:4, 8).

Do not be unequally yoked.

Ahab married a Canaanite woman who worshiped Baal. The Lord had expressly forbidden His people to intermarry with the Canaanites, and He expected His chosen king to lead the people by demonstrating obedience to His commands. Of course, Ahab was not the first king to sin in this way; Solomon took many foreign wives, and the end result was the same for both men: they were led away from the Lord by their unequal marriages.

Jezebel's influence over the king was profound, as we will see in later studies. As a priestess of Baal, she no doubt played an influential role in Ahab's decision to lead the entire nation into Baal worship and paganism. But this is no surprise, and it is part of the reason that the Lord commands His people to not marry unbelievers—for an unbelieving spouse will always exert an ungodly influence on the believer, and all too often will lead the believer far from obedience to His Word.

This principle applies today as much as it did in Ahab's time. Paul warns us, "Do not be unequally yoked together with unbelievers. For what fellowship has righteousness with lawlessness? And what communion has light with darkness? And what accord has Christ with Belial? Or what part has a believer with an unbeliever? And what agreement has the temple of God with idols? For you are the temple of the living God" (2 Corinthians 6:14–16).

The Lord provides for His people.

God sent a terrible drought upon Israel and the surrounding nations as a judgment for her sin of idolatry, but His servant Elijah never went hungry or thirsty. He did the same for the entire nation of Israel during her exodus from Egypt, providing water in the middle of the desert and food that miraculously rained from above. Even in the midst of His judgment on Ahab, the Lord would have ended the drought and restored His people if they had only repented of their idolatry.

This did not mean that Elijah suffered no hardship. He was called upon to live in the wilderness, depending upon ravens for food and a brook for water. The Lord even permitted him to face some uncertainty in His miraculous provision when the brook dried up. Yet Elijah's short-term difficulties were far outweighed by God's faithful provision, and he did not go hungry or thirsty.

The Lord has not changed since Elijah's day, and He still provides for His people today. All that He asks is that His people obey His Word and rely upon Him for our needs; He promises to take care of the rest. Jesus taught us, "Do not worry, saying, 'What shall we eat?' or 'What shall we drink?' or 'What shall we wear?' For after all these things the Gentiles seek. For your heavenly Father knows that you need all these things. But seek first the kingdom of God and His righteousness, and all these things shall be added to you" (Matthew 6:31–33).

5.   What does it mean to view sin as trivial? What sins does the world view as trivial today? Which ones have you sometimes viewed as trivial?

6.   What excuses might Ahab have offered for marrying Jezebel? What was God's view of that marriage?

7. What miraculous provisions did God make for His people throughout the Bible? What provisions has He made for you at times in your life?

8. If you had been in Elijah's place, how would you have felt about the drought? About the idolatry in Israel? About your situation living next to a brook?

9. *Are there areas of sin in your life that you choose to ignore? How does the Lord see those things? What do you need to do to gain God's perspective?*

10. *Make a list below of God's provisions for you; then take time to thank Him for His love and mercy.*

~ 5 ~
THE MINISTRY OF ELIJAH

∼ HISTORICAL BACKGROUND ∼

The drought had been going on for three and a half years, and the terrible lack of water had also precipitated a famine. Crops were dried up, livestock were dying, and the entire nation of Israel was suffering terribly. Ahab was trapped by his own folly. The longer he went worshiping Baal (the supposed god of rain), the more desperate he became and the more the Lord withheld the rain. But rather than repenting and turning to God, Ahab went on a desperate search for enough green grass to feed his remaining livestock. He and his servant split up in order to cover more ground. At this same time, the Lord informed Elijah that it was time to end the drought. Elijah obeyed the Lord's command to present himself before Ahab, and along the way he found Ahab's servant searching for grass. (That servant was Obadiah, whom we will get to know better in Study 8.) Elijah sent word to Ahab of God's intentions, and the king rushed cross-country to meet him.

But the problem that brought about the drought in the first place was still present in Israel, as neither Ahab nor the people had repented of their idolatry. So Elijah called for a dramatic confrontation: Bring together the prophets of Baal, and let them call upon their god to show his power. If Baal has any power, let the people serve him; otherwise, let the people turn back to the true God of Israel.

This is one of the most dramatic passages in the Old Testament, and it demonstrates how God alone controls the world. Israel was about to witness a vivid display of the power of their Creator.

∼ READING 1 KINGS 18:16–46 ∼

ENDING THE DROUGHT: *The Lord sends word to Elijah that it's time to end the drought, and Elijah obediently goes out to see King Ahab.*

16. OBADIAH: We will meet Obadiah in Study 8. He had been sent by Ahab to find grass for livestock during the famine—and he had met Elijah unexpectedly.

Ahab went to meet Elijah: This is a subtle but powerful statement. A king never went out to meet anyone, except perhaps another king; he would allow others to present themselves before him. But Ahab knew that Elijah was a true prophet of God, and that he had the authority to end the drought and famine, which had been going on for more than three years by this time. In his desperation, Ahab threw away kingly convention and rushed out to meet Elijah, even though the prophet was already on his way to the king.

17. O troubler of Israel: Ahab blamed Elijah for the drought, which was the opposite of the truth. It was God who had sent the drought, not Elijah, and it was Ahab who had moved the Lord's wrath in the first place. Ahab had the fool's habit of accusing others of his own sins.

18. you and your father's house have: Once again, Elijah spoke with amazing temerity. Ahab had accused him of a crime worthy of death, and he had the power to carry out that sentence if he chose. But Elijah knew that even the power of a king was nothing in the presence of God, and he did not fear Ahab's wrath. On the contrary, he boldly confronted the king with the truth, even though the truth would offend the king.

The Showdown: *Elijah tells Ahab to assemble the people of Israel on Mount Carmel, where they will see for themselves whether or not Baal can end their drought.*

19. gather all Israel to me: Elijah wanted the entire nation to be present for a clear demonstration that the God of Israel is the only one who rules the earth. His intention was to force the people to decide once and for all whom they would serve: Baal or Yahweh.

Mount Carmel: See the map in the Introduction for an approximate location. Carmel is actually a mountain range, not an isolated peak, noted for lush tree cover and fruitfulness. The effects of the drought were probably less there than in other areas, and Elijah may have selected this region in order to allow the priests of Baal every advantage in the coming "showdown." The Baal worshipers might think that their false god was at his greatest strength in such a place, and Baal's utter defeat would be all the more dramatic.

Asherah: Baal's consort, another false deity worshiped by the Canaanites.

who eat at Jezebel's table: Jezebel was a priestess to Baal, and she had surrounded herself with like-minded pagans. She took a personal interest in at least 850 priests of Baal and Asherah, and she had also slaughtered many prophets of God.

20. Ahab sent for all the children of Israel: It is interesting that Ahab, the king of Israel, obeyed the command of Elijah. He may have simply been motivated by a desire to end the drought one way or another, yet it is clear that he had gained respect for the power of God that was demonstrated in the prophet's life and words.

21. FALTER BETWEEN TWO OPINIONS: The word translated *falter* literally means to limp, but it is also used in verse 26 to mean "leap about" or "dance." The people of Israel were trying to jump back and forth between Baal and Yahweh, hoping to dance before two deities, but instead they were merely limping along like spiritual cripples.

FOLLOW HIM: Elijah was determined to force Israel to make a clear-cut choice between Baal and Yahweh. They were deluding themselves in the belief that they could intermingle the two religions into their own syncretistic blend, but God will not tolerate such adulteration of His Word. Either serve God with a whole heart, Elijah challenged, or limp away and chase after other gods—but stop trying to do both.

THE PEOPLE ANSWERED HIM NOT A WORD: Silence can be as condemning as words, and the people's refusal to answer merely underscored their stubborn determination to do things their own way.

22. I ALONE AM LEFT: Elijah was actually not the only prophet who spoke to Israel on the Lord's behalf, but he was alone on that mountaintop. He was emphasizing the fact that the entire nation had wandered away from the Lord, yet he was not daunted by being so outnumbered. Elijah's life was characterized by courage in speaking God's truth, whether anyone stood with him or not.

24. THE GOD WHO ANSWERS BY FIRE: Baal was supposed to wield control over thunder and lightning and storms, so if he was a true god, then this test was well within his power. The Lord, however, is the only One who controls the things of this world. He is the One "who makes the clouds His chariot, who walks on the wings of the wind, who makes His angels spirits, [and] His ministers a flame of fire" (Psalm 104:3–4).

ALL THE PEOPLE ANSWERED: Now at last the people of Israel have something to say. Seeing is believing, goes the old saying, and the people evidently thought that such a dramatic test would satisfy their doubts once and for all. But Jesus performed miracles far greater than this, and the people still crucified Him. "Now faith is the substance of things hoped for, the evidence of things not seen" (Hebrews 11:1).

BAAL'S TURN: *Elijah allows the false prophets to go first, and gives them the entire day to bring down fire from their nonexistent god. They fail.*

27. ELIJAH MOCKED THEM: Elijah's mockery actually followed many of the Baal myths, which described him as traveling or being deep in thought, yet the sarcasm must have hit home to the people of Israel. Despite the popular beliefs of the world around them, the truth was that Baal simply did not exist.

28. CUT THEMSELVES: Pagan worship practices included frenetic dancing (v. 26) and self-mutilation.

29. NO ONE PAID ATTENTION: Baal could not pay attention, since he didn't exist. In contrast, "the eyes of the LORD run to and fro throughout the whole earth, to show Himself strong on behalf of those whose heart is loyal to Him" (2 Chronicles 16:9).

GOD ACTS: *When the false priests are finally exhausted and bloody, Elijah steps up and repairs the altar of God. It's time for the people to see accurately who controls the heavens and earth.*

30. HE REPAIRED THE ALTAR OF THE LORD: This probably had been built in earlier days when the people of Israel still worshiped the Lord. It is significant that Elijah refused to touch the altar of Baal; instead, he literally rebuilt the worship practices that had been neglected by the people of God.

35. HE ALSO FILLED THE TRENCH WITH WATER: Elijah deliberately soaked both wood and sacrifice, even to the point of filling the surrounding trench with water, in order to make it abundantly clear that he was up to no tricks. No human agency would be able to ignite that sacrifice; only fire from heaven would accomplish it.

36. ELIJAH . . . SAID: Notice the sharp contrast between Elijah's simple prayer and the frenzied self-destruction of the false prophets. We do not need to perform dramatic acts to get God's attention—He is already attentive to His people. All that is required is that we speak to Him and listen to His Word.

40. SEIZE THE PROPHETS OF BAAL: God's law commanded that false prophets be put to death, as well as those who follow their false teachings (Deuteronomy 13:1–18).

41. THE SOUND OF ABUNDANCE OF RAIN: Elijah had such faith in God's promises that he sent Ahab away before there was even a cloud in the sky.

42. HE BOWED DOWN ON THE GROUND: Elijah's posture indicates both humility and repentance. He was humbling himself before God on behalf of the unfaithful nation of Israel, interceding on their behalf that the Lord would end the drought.

46. ELIJAH . . . RAN AHEAD OF AHAB: The distance between Carmel and Jezreel was roughly twenty miles—yet the Lord empowered Elijah to outrun the king's chariot! With God's prophet racing like the wind before him, and God's thunderous power roaring at his back, Ahab was once again forced to recognize that Jehovah was the only true God.

↶ First Impressions ↶

1. Why did Ahab call Elijah the "troubler of Israel" (v. 17)? Who was the real troublemaker?

2. Why did Elijah call for this dramatic confrontation with the prophets of Baal? Might there have been another way to confront the nation's idolatry?

3. Why did Elijah mock the prophets of Baal? What effect might his sarcasm have had on the false prophets? On the people of Israel who were spectators?

4.   *Why did Elijah have the false prophets slaughtered? What did this reveal about God's attitude toward idolatry? toward teachers of false religions?*

ᕁ Some Key Principles ᕁ

Do not fear what men might do.

Ahab was the king of Israel, and in that capacity he had the power to execute those whom he deemed his political enemies. This, in fact, was a very common practice in that day; many of the kings who preceded Ahab had ruthlessly slaughtered anyone who might have posed a potential threat to their power, even if those people had done nothing to provoke the king. Elijah had boldly come before Ahab and publicly condemned the king's wicked idolatry, and had further declared that the coming drought and famine would be lifted only when Elijah asked the Lord to do so. If ever Ahab had a public enemy, it was Elijah.

Yet this threat did not daunt Elijah, who continued to confront the king with boldness concerning his great sin of idolatry. Elijah knew that his life was in God's hands, and not even the king of Israel could harm a hair on his head without God's permission. Elijah's focus was entirely upon the sovereignty of God, and as a result he did not fear what men might do to him.

This is not an attitude of recklessness; God's people are not to act irresponsibly; neither are we to wantonly disobey those whom He has placed in authority over us. But Elijah had been sent to Ahab with a message from God, and he knew that his job was to obey God's command—regardless what Ahab might decide to do in retaliation. His priority was to do as he was told, and leave the consequences in God's hands. As the psalmist put it, "The LORD is on my side; I will not fear. What can man do to me?" (Psalm 118:6).

Be bold to speak God's truth, even when you are the only one.

Imagine how Elijah must have felt when he stood on Mount Carmel all by himself, facing 850 very hostile pagan priests, a powerful king who was looking for an excuse to execute him, and a crowd of Israelites who were indifferent at best to his fate. The entire nation had at least adulterated their worship practices with paganism, and the most powerful and influential in the land had embraced Baal outright. What's more, the 850 priests of Baal had official endorsement from the queen herself; they were the appointed leaders of the official state religion, and arguing against them was just not done.

Yet Elijah stood on the mountainside and did it—he argued loud and urgently against the false teachings of the world around him, even though nobody came up and stood beside him. Christians may find themselves in similar situations in modern times, especially as the world continues to move more openly into all manner of heathenism. For example, it can be intimidating to take a stand against the false doctrine of evolution; one can face open hostility and retribution for suggesting that God alone is the Creator of heaven and earth.

It is important to remember two things in this regard. First, Elijah may have felt alone, but he wasn't. The Lord had preserved a remnant in Israel of those who were faithful to Him, of those who refused to bow before Baal. Second, Elijah would not have been alone even if he *had* been the last faithful man in Israel—for he stood in the presence of the Almighty. The anger of those around him was ultimately not directed at Elijah; it was directed at God, and God would not ever abandon His devoted prophet. When we remember that we serve an omnipotent God who is always holding us in His hand, we will be encouraged to stand up boldly—even if we stand alone.

No one can serve two masters.

The people of Israel wanted to have multiple Gods. Many didn't want to completely abandon the God of Israel, perhaps because they enjoyed the many traditions and practices associated with worshiping Jehovah. But at the same time they also wanted to worship Baal, probably because it was unfashionable *not* to. In fact, with the endorsement of the king and queen, Baal worship was fast becoming expected of everyone in Israel, at least to some extent. So what was such a big deal about mixing the two together? A little bit of Baal, a dash of Yahweh, throw in a pinch of your favorite flavoring—and presto! One has a self-designed religion, guaranteed to fit one's needs and desires.

The problem is that there is, in eternal reality, only one God, and He has described Himself as "a jealous God" (Exodus 34:14)—He will not share men's worship with anything or anybody else. As we have seen in a previous study, it is possible to make idols out of almost anything in this world; when we allow something to become an idol, we effectively make it master of our life. Whatever we idolize will demand our time, attention, and energy, and this demand gives it mastery over us.

Money provides an excellent example of this pattern. We make money a priority when we begin to worry about tomorrow's expenses; when it becomes a priority, we begin to focus our attention on how to get more; when we focus on making money, our efforts begin to consume our energy and our time—and suddenly we discover that making money has become the driving force in our lives. Money has become an idol, and therefore our master. Jesus warned about this trap: "No one can serve two masters; for either he will hate the one and love the other, or else he will be loyal to the one and despise the other. You cannot serve God and mammon [money]" (Matthew 6:24). Jesus also taught His disciples the way out of this trap: "Therefore do not worry, saying, 'What shall we eat?' or 'What shall we drink?' or 'What shall we wear?' . . . But seek first the kingdom of God and His righteousness, and all these things shall be added to you" (Matthew 6:31, 33).

➳ DIGGING DEEPER ➳

5. Why did the people of Israel "falter between two opinions"? How did they get to that point? What was required to end their vacillation?

6. How was Elijah able to be so bold in his dealings with Ahab? Why did he not fear Ahab's wrath? How might his ministry have been different if he had been fearful?

7. What elements of God's wrath are demonstrated in this passage? What elements of His grace and mercy are demonstrated? How does His character display both justice and mercy in perfect balance?

8. What is so dangerous about intermingling Christianity with the teachings and practices of the world? How does this happen? How does it lead Christians away from God?

9. Is there anything in your life that threatens to become an idol (vying against the Lord for mastery)? What will you do this week to remove those threats?

10. When have you taken a bold stand for the Lord, even though you felt alone? What resulted from that stand? Is the Lord calling you to take such a stand at present?

SECTION 2:

CHARACTERS

In This Section:

⌁ CHARACTER'S BACKGROUND ⌁

The Lord had demonstrated His power and authority in a very dramatic way on Mount Carmel, and the truth about Baal's nonexistence had been revealed to the nation of Israel. The false prophets of Baal had been put to death, just as God's Word commanded, and the people of Israel had been brought to the point of choosing to serve God once and for all. Elijah's ministry had triumphed, and a day of revival was sure to follow.

At least that is what Elijah evidently thought—but Israel was so committed to paganism that not even the miraculous events of chapter 18 could turn the tide. Jezebel was still queen, and she was still not willing to bend her knee to the God of Israel. Moreover, Elijah was about to discover that she was not happy about the loss of her 850 favorite priests either. She had hardened her heart against the Lord, and even a dramatic miracle of fire from heaven was not going to move her to soften it.

Elijah viewed her opposition as a personal attack, and he could not understand how she could still reject the Lord. He became deeply discouraged, and his discouragement deepened into fear when Jezebel announced her intention to kill him. He fled the country, and his fear hit rock bottom when he despaired of his very life while hiding in the wilderness.

⌁ READING 1 KINGS 19:1–18 ⌁

THE WRATH OF JEZEBEL: *Ahab returns home and reports to his wife all that happened on Mount Carmel. Rather than turning away from Baal, however, she determines to kill Elijah.*

1. AHAB TOLD JEZEBEL ALL THAT ELIJAH HAD DONE: There is almost a sense here of subservience, as Ahab reports to his wife. There is no question that she took the leadership in their household (as we will see in our next study), and probably also in many political affairs.

2. MAKE YOUR LIFE AS THE LIFE OF ONE OF THEM: It is interesting that Ahab took no apparent interest in the fate of the 850 false prophets—but Jezebel certainly did. It was through her efforts that further persecution broke out against Elijah and other prophets of God. This suggests once again the influence that she had over the king's idolatrous practices. Even after the dramatic demonstration of God's power and Baal's nonexistence, she still refused to repent of her idolatry. Like Pharaoh in Egypt, she had completely hardened her heart against the Lord, and no display of His presence and power would move her to humble herself before Him.

3. RAN FOR HIS LIFE: It is hard to understand why the bold prophet who confronted kings and called down fire from heaven and slaughtered false prophets would suddenly turn and flee from Jezebel. It is true that she was far more likely to carry out her threats against his life than Ahab was, but we have already seen how Elijah placed his trust firmly in God's sovereign hand. But Israel's disbelief was too much for him to bear, and he became dejected. James reminds us that "Elijah was a man with a nature like ours" (James 5:17); he was subject to the same human weaknesses as everyone else.

4. BROOM TREE: A desert bush that grew to approximately ten feet in height.

IT IS ENOUGH: Elijah had spent the past three and a half years in hiding, and now his nation had rejected him despite the fact that the Lord had used him to end the drought. Elijah was focused on how people responded to his ministry, rather than on the fact that the Lord had used him. This is a surefire recipe for discouragement, and even the great prophet was no exception.

TAKE MY LIFE: Yet even in his despair, Elijah recognized that his life was in God's hands—even though he had temporarily forgotten this fact in the face of Jezebel's threats. He no longer wanted to continue in his lonely ministry, and he was asking God to end his life.

I AM NO BETTER THAN MY FATHERS: Israel's spiritual leaders had all faced rejection from their own people. Samuel was rejected in favor of a king, and even Moses felt distressed because of Israel's stubbornness (Numbers 11:1–5; 1 Samuel 8:7). Elijah was no different.

GOD PROVIDES FOR HIS SERVANT: *Elijah is overcome with misery and exhaustion, but an angel of God appears to provide him sustenance.*

5. AN ANGEL TOUCHED HIM: Often, in times of weakness, the Lord sends angels to minister to His people. This happened to Moses, and even to Jesus Himself (Matthew 4:11; Acts 7:35).

6. CAKE . . . WATER: The Lord met Elijah's needs as He did at Cherith, but this time the food was delivered by the hand of an angel rather than the beaks of ravens. The Lord was keeping him alive in order to bring him to Mount Horeb.

7. THE JOURNEY IS TOO GREAT FOR YOU: The Lord knows the limitations of His servants better than they do. Elijah thought that he'd reached the end of his strength, but the Lord still had more for him to accomplish. For those times when the work did actually exceed Elijah's capabilities, the Lord provided miraculous sustenance that enabled him to accomplish it.

8. FORTY DAYS AND FORTY NIGHTS: Moses spent forty days and nights on Mount Sinai (Exodus 24:18), and Jesus spent forty days and nights in the wilderness (Matthew 4:2). The Lord ministered to the needs of His servants in those instances as well.

HOREB: That is, Mount Sinai, approximately two hundred miles south of Beersheba. The Lord was bringing Elijah to the very place where Moses was charged with giving the Law to the Jews. Not only did this place represent the Law, but it represented the fact that God had chosen a leader to bring His people into their land. Now that Elijah had been rejected by the people, he came to this place to seek the Lord.

THE STILL SMALL VOICE: *The Lord meets with Elijah on Mount Horeb and teaches him an important lesson. He also encourages His servant and sends him back to his ministry.*

9. WHAT ARE YOU DOING HERE: Evidently Elijah had gone to Mount Horeb on his own initiative, rather than at the Lord's command. The Lord had appeared to Moses on the same mountain, and it is possible that Elijah wanted to meet with God in the same manner. (There are many parallels between the ministry of Moses and that of Elijah.)

10. I HAVE BEEN VERY ZEALOUS: Elijah was not in a fit of self-pity as much as he was simply shocked at how unbelieving Israel had become. The situation was so bad that Elijah had gone back to Egypt, as if he wanted the Lord to forget about Israel and start over with a new people in a new place.

THE CHILDREN OF ISRAEL HAVE FORSAKEN YOUR COVENANT: Moses faced a similar situation when he came down from Mount Sinai and found the people worshiping a golden calf, and he responded with intercession before the Lord on behalf of Israel (Exodus 32:11–13). Moses remembered that the Lord is in control of all things, and that He loved the people of Israel deeply; Elijah had interceded for his people back at Mount Carmel, and now he despaired over their unbelief. He saw no hope for Israel's future.

I ALONE AM LEFT: Strictly speaking, there were other Israelites who had not worshiped Baal. Yet Elijah did not know any of them, and so he appealed to God for help. The Lord assured him that the words were not true.

11–12. WIND . . . EARTHQUAKE . . . FIRE: The Lord's presence was frequently indicated in the Old Testament by such destructive forces, indicating His power or His wrath—yet they do not summarize His character. God is powerful and just, but He is also gentle and merciful. Elijah's ministry had been focused on God's justice and His wrath against Israel's unfaithfulness, but now he was going to learn about God's love and mercy.

12. A STILL SMALL VOICE: God does work in dramatic ways, sometimes showing His terrifying power and fury. But He also works in quiet, gentle ways, and He wanted Elijah to see that the time for judgment had not yet come. The Lord was quietly at work in the lives of many people within Israel, even during those dark days.

13. WHAT ARE YOU DOING HERE: The Lord repeated His previous question, and Elijah repeated his previous answer verbatim.

15–16. HAZAEL . . . JEHU . . . ELISHA: These three men would complete the work that Elijah began, effectively rooting out Baal worship from Israel. While Elijah had tried to abandon Israel, the Lord was sending him back with a task—he was to hand off his ministry to others.

18. ALL WHOSE KNEES HAVE NOT BOWED TO BAAL: The Lord assured Elijah that He was still powerfully at work in the lives of His people, preserving seven thousand who had not been seduced by idolatry. Such power is often not dramatic, which is what the Lord was showing Elijah in the still small voice, but it is no less the powerful work of God.

✌ FIRST IMPRESSIONS ✌

1. *If you had been in Elijah's place, how might you have expected Jezebel to react to the events on Mount Carmel? If you had been in her place, how might you have responded?*

2. *Why did Elijah flee to the wilderness? What did he hope to find there? What did he actually find?*

3. *What caused Elijah's despair? If you had been in his place, how might you have felt? What might you have done?*

4. *Why did God not allow Elijah to leave Israel permanently? What might God have been trying to help Elijah see?*

.

↜ Some Key Principles ↝

God is sovereign even when His message is rejected.

What a dramatic contrast we see in this chapter between Elijah's bold courage on Mount Carmel and his discouraged hopelessness on Mount Horeb. It is easy to understand why he was so distraught—fire from heaven, the great victory over the priests of Baal, the dramatic run from Carmel to Jezreel, the joyful end to the drought—all of this should have caused the Israelites to repent and serve the Lord. But instead, Jezebel wanted Elijah dead, and the Israelites did not defend him.

Elijah's words reveal the deeper source of his despair: he thought he was the only true follower of Yahweh left, and he was jealous for God's glory. Elijah had his focus on

Jezebel's rejection of God and the people's failure to overthrow the false religion of Baal, and he could not reconcile that rejection with the idea of a sovereign God.

Yet God is still in control, even when His message is rejected. Elijah needed to remember that Moses was likewise rejected, and the Lord still brought His people into Israel, albeit forty years later. Elijah was not allowed to walk away, because the Lord was not done with him yet. Christians are called to be faithful evangelists, yet at the same time we are powerless to save anyone. While the world may reject the message, God still remains in control.

We live in the age of grace—but the day of God's wrath is coming.

Elijah's ministry was characterized by great drama. He prayed, and the Lord closed the heavens, sending a terrible drought and famine that lasted more than three years. He prayed again, and the Lord opened the heavens. He prayed another time, and the Lord sent down fire, which consumed everything in its path. Yet God also wanted him to learn about His still, less visible ways.

The Lord's message to Elijah on Mount Horeb was that He was powerfully at work in Israel even when the fire and fury were not raining down. He works constantly in the lives and hearts of people today through His Holy Spirit and His Word; He has provided incalculable grace through the death and resurrection of His Son Jesus. We live in this age of grace today, and we gain eternal life and forgiveness of sin as a free gift, simply through faith in Jesus Christ.

But Christians also must not lose sight of the fact that the day of grace will come to an end—and after that will come God's terrible judgment. Elijah was not wrong when he anticipated that God would move through the fire and earthquake; it was just not the complete picture. God is merciful and gracious, but He is also just—and in the day of His justice, there will be dreadful fire and sorrow. "We then," warns the apostle Paul, "as workers together with Him also plead with you not to receive the grace of God in vain. For He says: 'In an acceptable time I have heard you, and in the day of salvation I have helped you.' Behold, now is the accepted time; behold, now is the day of salvation" (2 Corinthians 6:1–2).

The Lord takes care of His own.

During the terrible drought and famine, the Lord provided Elijah with food and water. When he was completely exhausted, He provided more sustenance. Moses received the same provisions during the forty days and nights that he spent on Mount Sinai, and

Jesus was sustained by the Father during His forty days in the wilderness. The people of Israel enjoyed manna and quail during their sojourn in the desert, and the Lord miraculously supplied water from rocks when they needed it.

And the Lord's provision is not restricted to our physical needs. He knew that Elijah needed to refocus his attention on the character of God and get his eyes off himself, so He gave him a personal demonstration of His gentleness and grace, which was just what His servant needed at the time. He knew that the work in Israel was too large for Elijah, so He brought along others to carry on for him. He did the same for Moses when His servant was overcome with discouragement (Numbers 11:15–17).

The Lord understands the human frame better than anyone; He created it from dust, and He also took on human form Himself and experienced firsthand what it means to be a man. He provides for His servants' needs because He understands those needs—better than we do ourselves—and because He loves each of His children deeply. Jesus understood our need for God's help, and He sent us the ultimate Helper (or Comforter) in the person of the Holy Spirit. "And I will pray the Father," He said before His ascension, "and He will give you another Helper, that He may abide with you forever—the Spirit of truth, whom the world cannot receive, because it neither sees Him nor knows Him; but you know Him, for He dwells with you and will be in you. I will not leave you orphans; I will come to you" (John 14:16–18).

⌁ Digging Deeper ⌁

5. *What do the wind, earthquake, and fire reveal about God's character? Why was He not in them during His encounter with Elijah?*

6. *What does the still small voice reveal about God's character? Why did He choose that to communicate with Elijah? What was He teaching His servant?*

7. How did discouragement influence Elijah's actions and attitudes in this chapter? When have you experienced similar discouragement or despair? How has it affected your actions and attitudes?

8. How can you maintain your trust in God's sovereignty, even while people are rejecting His message?

ᴛ Taking It Personally ᴛ

9. Do you know someone who is struggling with discouragement? How can you act as a "ministering angel" to help that person?

10. How has the Lord provided for you in the past week? Make a list below of His recent provisions; then spend time in prayer and thanksgiving.

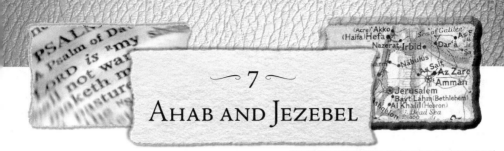

~ 7 ~
AHAB AND JEZEBEL

⌁ CHARACTERS' BACKGROUND ⌁

Sometime after the events on Mount Carmel, the king of Syria gathered a huge army and attacked Israel. (See 1 Kings 20 for the full account of these events.) The Syrians were a world superpower, and their army vastly outnumbered that of the Israelites. But the Lord sent word to Ahab that He intended to give Israel a great victory over Syria, for the express purpose that the people of Israel would see once again that He was their God, and that He alone could save them.

As promised, the Lord gave Israel a mighty victory over Syria in a very short battle fought in the hills and valleys surrounding Samaria. The king of Syria, however, did not learn his lesson; he determined that Israel's God had won a victory because He was God of the hills. Therefore, he led his army against Israel once again, but this time determined to fight on the open plains, where Israel's God would have no authority. So the Lord sent a prophet to Ahab once again, telling him that He would utterly defeat Syria once and for all, demonstrating to all the world that He is God of all creation. And once again, the Lord kept His word, delivering the entire Syrian army into Israel's hands.

And then Ahab disobeyed the Lord once again. His job was to put to death the king of Syria, but instead he made a treaty and sent the king back to Syria in peace. The Lord sent His prophet one more time, but this time he bore a dire message for Ahab, informing him that God would demand his life in exchange for the king of Syria. Ahab went home "sullen and displeased" (1 Kings 20:43), but things were about to get worse.

⌁ READING 1 KINGS 21:1–29 ⌁

COVETING A VINEYARD: *King Ahab looks out his window and sees his neighbor's vineyard—and decides that he must have it. But the neighbor won't sell.*

1. AFTER THESE THINGS: Ben-Hadad, the king of Syria, had made war against Israel. The Lord had caused Israel to triumph gloriously, demonstrating for all the world that He is Lord of all the earth. The Lord had commanded Ahab to execute Ben-Hadad after the battle, but Ahab allowed himself to be bribed and gave the king his freedom. The Lord then sent a prophet to Ahab, telling him that his life would be forfeited for his failure to obey God's commands.

2. GIVE ME YOUR VINEYARD: The Canaanite nations around Israel commonly bought and sold land, much as we do in modern culture. The Israelites, however, did not sell their land, out of obedience to God's commands, and one would expect the king of Israel to understand this. But Ahab had been so strongly influenced by his wife's Canaanite ways that he had adopted them for himself, and evidently he expected the people of Israel to adopt them as well. Rather than leading God's people in obedience to the Lord's commands, Ahab was leading Israel into the ways of the pagans.

3. THE LORD FORBID: The Lord had commanded Israel to not buy and sell their property in Canaan, because the land was the Lord's, and He wanted His people to be "strangers and sojourners" there (Leviticus 25:23–28). Each tribe and family had received an allotment of land, and it was to be viewed as a permanent heritage, not to be sold or bartered away. Naboth stood in stark contrast to the king when he refused to disobey the Lord's commands, and his obedience shamed Ahab.

A ROYAL TEMPER TANTRUM: *Ahab's response to not getting his way typifies his character, as he stomps into his bedroom and refuses to eat.*

4. SULLEN AND DISPLEASED: Ahab was pouting because Naboth's obedience to the Lord's directives had highlighted his own disobedience. Notice how childish Ahab's behavior is, as he lies on his bed, pouting and refusing to eat, like a surly, spoiled brat. This is the king of Israel, the same king who had recently led the nation of Israel into a miraculous rout against a more powerful enemy. This underscores the fact that Israel's victory over Syria was entirely the Lord's doing, and it also shows the true nature of stubborn disobedience. Those who refuse to obey the Word of God are actually like Ahab, stubborn children who pout when they can't have their own way.

5. JEZEBEL HIS WIFE: The author of 1 Kings frequently refers to Jezebel as Ahab's wife, reminding us of Ahab's sin of marrying such a heathen in the first place.

6. BECAUSE I SPOKE TO NABOTH THE JEZREELITE: One can almost hear the pout in Ahab's voice.

7. YOU NOW EXERCISE AUTHORITY OVER ISRAEL: It's a sad commentary that Ahab, the king of God's chosen people, had to be rebuked for his childlike behavior by a committed pagan who hated the Lord and had murdered hundreds of His prophets.

I will give you the vineyard: Once again, Jezebel takes the helm of leadership both in Ahab's household and over the nation of Israel.

Jezebel Takes Charge: *The queen steps in on her husband's behalf and hatches a wicked plot to cheat Naboth out of his land—and his life.*

8. she wrote letters in Ahab's name: This clearly demonstrates the degree to which Jezebel exercised authority over Israel. The king's seal indicated absolute royal authority to any decree, and it was not used by anyone except the king himself. When a king permitted another person to use his seal in this way, it indicated an absolute trust; the person so entrusted was acting in the place of the king.

9. Proclaim a fast: Calling upon the people to humble themselves and fast implied that the Lord was sending a judgment upon them. The people would have assumed that there was some grievous sin in their midst and would be quick to put to death whoever the culprit was (Joshua 7). This is a terrific irony, since there actually *was* grievous sin in Israel—the sin of Baal worship—but it was not faithful men like Naboth who were responsible.

13. they took him outside the city and stoned him with stones: Here is yet another bitter irony: the people of Israel refused to obey the Lord's commands concerning idolatry, yet they carefully followed the law when they stoned an innocent man by taking him outside the city gates. They also murdered his sons (2 Kings 9:26), effectively removing all his heirs.

14. Then they sent to Jezebel: The fact that the elders contacted Jezebel rather than the king might suggest that they knew the plot was from her hand, even though the orders had been sealed by the king's signet. This and the fact that they murdered Naboth's sons suggest that the elders of the city were complicit in this wicked crime.

The Lord's Judgment Falls: *The Lord sends Elijah to inform Ahab that God's wrath is about to fall upon his household. The Lord had warned of such judgment in His Law.*

18. There he is: Ahab and Jezebel thought that they could hide their wicked deeds, but the Lord saw all that they did. God was watching Ahab enter Naboth's vineyard, even as He was sending Elijah to meet him.

19. dogs shall lick your blood: Ahab repented when he heard Elijah's dire warning, so the Lord did not carry out this prophecy—not entirely. Dogs did end up licking Ahab's blood, but it happened in another location (1 Kings 22:37–38).

20. O MY ENEMY: This is the mind-set of a man who has hardened his heart to the Lord. Elijah was not Ahab's enemy; he was actually trying to turn the king away from his path of self-destruction, as well as the entire nation of Israel. But Ahab could only see that Elijah was opposing his stubborn self-will.

YOU HAVE SOLD YOURSELF: Ahab didn't realize that he had, in fact, sold his soul in exchange for short-term gains. "For what profit is it to a man," our Lord asked, "if he gains the whole world, and loses his own soul? Or what will a man give in exchange for his soul?" (Matthew 16:26).

22. LIKE THE HOUSE OF JEROBOAM: The Lord had pronounced this same judgment on Jeroboam (1 Kings 14:10–11), and it was the fulfillment of His dire warning to the people dating back to the law of Moses: if Israel chased after false gods, the Lord would send calamity upon them (Deuteronomy 28). This calamity would end, the Lord warned, in Israel being taken into captivity (vv. 63–64), which ultimately proved true.

BAASHA: An earlier king. See 1 Kings 16:2–4.

23. CONCERNING JEZEBEL: Jezebel was the only queen singled out for judgment in the long list of wicked kings in Israel. She had taken authority on herself, both in her home and in the nation, so the Lord held her to the same level of accountability as He did the king.

24. THE DOGS SHALL EAT: The final disgrace is to die and remain unburied, so that birds and wild animals devour one's remains. Yet the Lord had warned of this consequence when His people chased after false gods (Deuteronomy 28:26).

25. BECAUSE JEZEBEL HIS WIFE STIRRED HIM UP: Ahab was capable of being strong and courageous, such as when leading his army into battle. But at home he was weak and contemptible, permitting his wife to take the headship—and her headship ultimately reached beyond their home to include Ahab's kingly authority. He might have been a very different king if he had not disobeyed the Lord's injunction against marrying foreign wives.

27. HE TORE HIS CLOTHES: Ahab's actions were outward displays of grief and mourning, and his repentance was genuine, although not complete (see 1 Kings 22). Unfortunately, it was too late, for the Lord's judgment had already come upon him. His repentance may have bought him some time, but it did not remove the consequences of his sin.

29. IN THE DAYS OF HIS SON: Ahab's son Joram died in Naboth's field (2 Kings 9:24–26). Because of Ahab's repentance, the Lord delayed His judgment on him. But Ahab's line would end in the days of his son.

ᔈ Reading 2 Kings 9:30–37 ᔈ

Jezebel's Bitter End: *Jehu becomes king over Israel, and carries out his duties in fulfilling the Lord's judgment on the house of Ahab. Jezebel remains unrepentant to the very end.*

30. Jehu: As we saw in our last study, the Lord had told Elijah to anoint Jehu as king over Israel. That duty was actually fulfilled by Elisha, Elijah's successor. The Lord had also commanded Jehu to overthrow Ahab's son Joram, who was king at this time. Ahab was already dead, but Jezebel lived on.

she put paint on her eyes: Jezebel probably recognized that her end was upon her, yet she remained defiant and arrogant to the last, even taking time to put on makeup as her execution drew near.

31. Zimri: Zimri had overthrown King Elah (1 Kings 16:11–12) and stolen the throne, but he only sat on that throne for seven days. Jezebel was suggesting that Jehu had done the same thing, and that he would meet the same end. She was wrong.

ᔈ First Impressions ᔈ

1. Why did Ahab want Naboth's vineyard in the first place? What would he have gained by owning it? What does this reveal about Ahab's character?

2. Why did Naboth refuse to sell his land? What might he have gained by selling? What did he lose by refusing? What does this reveal about Naboth's priorities?

3. How did Jezebel's solution to the vineyard problem compare with Ahab's solution? How might her idolatry have influenced her approach to the problem?

4. What was the result of Naboth's faithfulness to God's commands? What does this teach about the Christian life? about the potential for suffering when we follow Christ?

ꝏ Some Key Principles ꝏ

Coveting is a form of idolatry.

Ahab looked out from his mighty palace and noticed an insignificant piece of property nearby. It was a neighbor's vineyard—nothing fancy or large, just a nice little piece of land that would be suitable for a vegetable garden. Perhaps Ahab had developed a sudden urge to take up gardening; perhaps he just developed a sudden craving for the land simply because he didn't own it. Whatever his reasons, he suddenly began to covet that land above all things.

It seems odd at first glance that the king of Israel, who had immense wealth and power, should work himself into a lather over a vegetable garden. But Ahab was an idolater; he had forsaken the one true God of heaven and earth in favor of a piece of wood made by men—he had forsaken the Creator in favor of the creation—and it was only natural that he should continue to set his heart upon the things of this earth.

The Bible is clear that covetousness is the same as idolatry. We begin to covet when we set our hearts and minds upon the material and temporal things of this world, rather than on the eternal things of God, and this is a form of idolatry, putting other things at higher priority than the Lord. When we find ourselves coveting, the only solution is to refocus our minds onto the Lord and His Word. "For this you know," warns Paul, "that no fornicator, unclean person, nor covetous man, *who is an idolater*, has any inheritance in the kingdom of Christ and God" (Ephesians 5:5, emphasis added).

Obedience to God's Word sometimes leads to suffering— but it's still the best plan.

As king of Israel, Ahab of all people should have understood that the people of Israel were not permitted to sell their land. The land belonged to God, and He had allotted portions to the families of Israel; He expected them to keep their inheritance as a sacred trust from Him. Naboth did understand this, and he stood firm in his obedience to God's commands—even to the point of refusing the king!

Yet Naboth suffered for his obedience, and paid the ultimate price for his faithfulness—he and all his sons with him. He did not find a "happy ending" to his story; instead, he was stoned to death outside the city walls, as though he had committed some great blasphemy against God. This was the grossest injustice, yet it was Naboth's fate when he obeyed the Word of God.

But we have not yet read the end of the story, which will unfold when we meet the Lord in eternity. At that time, Naboth will receive a great reward for his faithfulness, as will all who suffer injustice for obedience to God. The Lord does permit His servants to suffer for being faithful—after all, Jesus suffered the grossest injustice of all men when He died for living a sinless life. Jesus warned us of the potential for suffering: "If the world hates you, you know that it hated Me before it hated you. If you were of the world, the world would love its own. Yet because you are not of the world, but I chose you out of the world, therefore the world hates you. Remember the word that I said to you, 'A servant is not greater than his master.' If they persecuted Me, they will also persecute you" (John 15:18–20).

When we disobey God, we sell out our soul to sin.

Ahab wanted Naboth's vineyard; Naboth wouldn't sell. Ahab bartered and pleaded; Naboth stood firm. Ahab pouted; Naboth ignored him. So the mighty king of Israel, who had just won an amazing military victory against a world superpower, stomped off to his bedroom to sulk. He threw himself on his bed, turned his face to the wall, and pettishly refused to eat any food. Ahab threw a temper tantrum, but when Elijah confronted him, notice how Elijah described Ahab's sin: "You have sold yourself to do evil" (1 Kings 21:20).

Ahab had murdered in exchange for a vineyard. In 1 Kings 20, he had ignored the Lord's command in exchange for a bribe. The Lord describes both of these sins as a form of selling out. Ahab had a choice: obey God, or forfeit his loyalty to fulfill his sinful desires. He wanted a vineyard, so he allowed his wife to murder an innocent man.

When a person sins, he is saying that there is something he desires more than obedience to God. He is saying that a certain pleasure, or in this case a vineyard, will bring more joy than the joy that comes from obedience. Sin is the selling out of our soul. It has been said that every man has a price; in Ahab's case, he sold out for a vineyard. He desired sin, and he sold himself to serve it. This is what it means to be a slave to sin. When a person sells his loyalty in exchange for sin, he becomes a servant to sin, and an enemy to God.

5. How did Jezebel gain such power and influence in Israel? How might things have been different if Ahab had not married her?

6. What did the Lord mean when He said that Ahab had sold himself (1 Kings 21:20)? In what sense had he done this? What led him to it? What resulted?

7. In what ways is coveting the same as idol worship? How did Ahab's idolatry lead him to covet his neighbor's land? How did idolatry lead him to murder?

8. How is contentment different from happiness? How does a person gain contentment? Read Philippians 4:11–13. How did Paul gain contentment?

ᔰ Taking It Personally ᔰ

9. Are there any idols in your life? Are you presently coveting something (or someone) that you don't possess? How will you root out this sin?

10. List below some of God's blessings in your life, and spend time thanking Him for them. Repeat this each day for the coming week, asking Him to teach you contentment.

～ 8 ～
OBADIAH

1 KINGS 18

～ CHARACTER'S BACKGROUND ～

In the ancient Near East, kings were very powerful and wealthy, and their households were filled with servants. Being a king was a consuming job, and kings did not have time to manage the complicated domestic affairs within their own households, so they would appoint a man to be in charge of all the servants and requirements of the home. This man was known as the *steward*, and he carried a heavy load of responsibility.

In addition to overseeing a miniature army of servants, the steward also had to guard the king's life. It was fairly easy in those days to poison a king, for example, since the people preparing the food were far removed from the king's presence. So the steward was also a food taster who tested everything that the king ate to ensure that it was safe.

Obviously, the king would only appoint a man whom he trusted deeply to such a position. The steward was more than a bodyguard, though. He would have to possess a wide array of organizational skills, a sense of diplomacy, an understanding of policy, and the ability to manage not just the servants and the king's family but also the affairs of the nation. To rise to such a position of prominence and responsibility, a man needed to be both diligent and skillful.

Such a man was Obadiah, steward of King Ahab. But Obadiah's position was even more demanding than that of most stewards, because he was also devoted to the Lord while serving in the household of Israel's most wicked and idolatrous king. Obadiah's very life was in constant danger, since Queen Jezebel was making it a point to eradicate all God's faithful followers from the land—and Ahab's steward would have been no exception.

In this study, we will learn what it means to be a diligent and faithful servant of God, and we will also see an example of quiet courage in action. Obadiah did not flee from his dangerous situation; in fact, he made it more dangerous still by saving the lives of the prophets whom Jezebel sought to destroy.

❧ READING 1 KINGS 18:1–15 ❧

ENDING THE DROUGHT: *We now return to the time just prior to Elijah's confrontation on Mount Carmel. The Lord has told him that He will end the drought, and he goes to meet Ahab.*

1. AFTER MANY DAYS: We have now moved back in time to the great drought that Elijah predicted in Israel. The drought had been going on for three and a half years (James 5:17), and the confrontation on Mount Carmel had yet to take place.

I WILL SEND RAIN ON THE EARTH: The Lord had given Elijah the authority to call for the end of the drought (1 Kings 17:1), but here we are reminded that only the Lord had control over the natural forces of the earth. Elijah understood this, but most Israelites did not; they had turned themselves to the worship of Baal, believing that a fictitious god could control the rains and harvests of the earth.

3. OBADIAH: The name means "servant of the Lord." This is not the same man who wrote the Old Testament book of Obadiah. He was a high-ranking servant of the king "who was in charge of his house," meaning that he was Ahab's steward. He would have been a highly trusted official with substantial authority within the king's household.

A QUIETLY COURAGEOUS MAN: *Obadiah is the steward of Ahab's household, a very important position in the kingdom. But he is also a servant of the Most High God.*

OBADIAH FEARED THE LORD GREATLY: This statement is very significant, considering that he was a trusted servant within the home of Jezebel, a woman who hated God's people to the point that she murdered His prophets. It demonstrates that the Lord is capable of placing His servants wherever He chooses, even under the very noses of His enemies. It also suggests that Obadiah's faithfulness to the Lord extended also to his work and his employers. They trusted him because he was faithful to his duties, and this is a mark of one who is obedient to the Lord's commands.

4. JEZEBEL MASSACRED THE PROPHETS OF THE LORD: We are not told how many of God's people were murdered at the hand of Jezebel, but the fact that Obadiah saved one hundred suggests that she slaughtered many more than that. The word translated "massacred" literally means to cut off or eliminate. Jezebel was attempting to utterly annihilate the people of God who opposed Baal, to cut off and eliminate the Lord's people from the land. Her hatred of God was profound, and she was utterly determined to destroy any who worshiped Him. Obadiah lived in a dangerous situation.

FIFTY TO A CAVE: The area around Carmel includes thousands of caves, many of which are large enough to hold fifty men.

FED THEM WITH BREAD AND WATER: While ravens had been feeding Elijah at the brook, Obadiah had been performing the same service for other prophets. Here we discover that Elijah had not been the only servant of the Lord remaining when he thought he was (1 Kings 19:10), and that the Lord had been just as faithful in providing for His other servants as He had been to Elijah.

> **AN UNEXPECTED MEETING:** *Obadiah suddenly encounters Elijah in the wilderness, and he is pleased—at first. But then he is filled with fear at what he must do next.*

6. THEY DIVIDED THE LAND BETWEEN THEM: Here is another powerful testimony to the trust that Ahab placed in Obadiah. The king felt that the job was so important that he was willing to walk throughout Israel by himself in search of grass for his livestock, so he would have selected only the most competent and trustworthy man to cover the other half.

7. SUDDENLY ELIJAH MET HIM: Elijah's sudden appearance probably startled Obadiah. Elijah was a wanted man, and this encounter would put Obadiah in an awkward position. Would he arrest him and bring him to Ahab, or would he honor him as a prophet?

FELL ON HIS FACE: Obadiah was a very important man in Israel, and he wielded considerable authority as steward of the king's household. Yet he humbled himself to the point of falling on his face before Elijah, demonstrating his deep respect for the Lord's servants. He probably also showed respect for the king by virtue of his office as the Lord's chosen king over Israel, but he also did not put stock in the trappings of the world—he was ready to abase himself before those who stood in the presence of the King of kings.

9. HOW HAVE I SINNED: Obadiah's fear is that Ahab will suddenly suspect him of some sort of treachery, thinking that he is in league with Elijah in some devious plot against his throne. This, of course, was the opposite of the truth, as God's servants were trying to turn the king back to obedience to His commands, thus saving both the king and the nation. But those who have hardened their hearts against the Lord fear treachery at every turn, for they themselves are treacherous to God.

12. THE SPIRIT OF THE LORD WILL CARRY YOU: Obadiah was also afraid that, once he had told Ahab where to find Elijah, the Lord would whisk him away to some distant place. Ahab would then explode in irrational anger and kill his servant. Obadiah viewed himself as being between a rock and a hard place: he was afraid that Elijah would play a trick on him, and he was afraid that Ahab would kill him regardless. He had previously been very courageous in saving the prophets of God, but he had done that secretly; now the Lord was calling him to take action publicly.

13. Was it not reported to my lord: Obadiah seems to have lost sight of the fact that God saw all his deeds, and that He would not abandon His faithful servant. He evidently felt the need to remind God of what he had done, fearing that the Lord would not protect him otherwise. His fear caused him to think that he had to earn God's favor, when the truth was just the opposite. This thinking did not characterize his life, however; it was the fear of the moment that caused him to speak this way, coupled with the fact that this step of faith could not be carried out clandestinely.

⌒ First Impressions ⌒

1. *Why did Ahab personally walk through the land, looking for grass? What did it reveal about Obadiah that Ahab entrusted the task to him as well?*

2. *What risks did Obadiah take when he hid one hundred prophets in caves? Why did he do this?*

3. *Why did Elijah's request make Obadiah afraid? What did he fear? What caused those fears?*

4. *If you had been in Obadiah's place, what would you have done when Jezebel started murdering prophets? How would you have responded to Elijah's request?*

⌁ Some Key Principles ⌁

Whatever the Lord gives you to do, do it with all your might.

Obadiah had risen to a great height in his career. The king's steward held a position of tremendous trust and authority, as the king generally gave him full responsibility over his entire household. Indeed, the king trusted his very life to his steward, since one of the steward's responsibilities was to ensure that nobody poisoned the king's food. Obadiah had no doubt attained this position, from a human perspective, by virtue of diligent and skillful work. Whatever Obadiah did, he did it well.

But there is another side to this situation that must not be overlooked. The truth is that Obadiah had been placed in this important position by the Lord, and at least part of God's reason for placing him there was so that he could save the lives of the prophets during Jezebel's murderous spree. And here again Obadiah's diligent habits came into play: he saw an opportunity to serve the Lord, and he took full advantage of it. You might say that Obadiah was given the work of saving lives, and he saved those lives with all his might.

Obadiah was a servant to a king, and he ensured that his work was fit for a king. Christians should cultivate this same attitude, for we are servants to the King of kings. Whatever we are called to do, even the most mundane responsibilities, we should strive to make our work fit for the King. "Whatever you do," Paul wrote, "do it heartily, as to the Lord and not to men, knowing that from the Lord you will receive the reward of the inheritance; for you serve the Lord Christ" (Colossians 3:23–24).

The Lord sees our actions, and He knows who belongs to Him.

Jezebel's murder of the prophets called for a clandestine response. Obadiah could not openly hide them, since she would have simply killed him and taken the prophets as well. But when Elijah called him to take an open stand for the Lord, he panicked, fearing that the prophet might play a mean trick on him. Obadiah suddenly began to wonder whether the Lord had noticed his previous acts of obedience, and he feared that God might hand him over to His enemies. His fear (which we will cover in our next principle) caused him to momentarily forget the character of God.

The truth was that the Lord had indeed seen Obadiah's bravery and obedience, and He knew the condition of his heart—even better than Obadiah himself did. The Lord had His hand on His servant, and He was carefully guiding all the events of his life. It was no coincidence that Elijah suddenly appeared before him, even though Obadiah was intent upon a completely different task. Indeed, it was no coincidence that Obadiah was Ahab's steward in the first place, as we discussed in our previous principle. Obadiah belonged securely to the Lord, and He was directing all the events that came into his life.

There are times when the Lord wants His children to obey Him, even in costly ways, when nobody else is watching. But He is watching, and He takes pleasure in seeing our acts of worship and obedience that are done in secret. Jesus reiterated this principle repeatedly in Matthew 6, where He said many times, "your Father who sees in secret will reward you openly." Obadiah had nothing to fear, and neither have we.

Be courageous.

Obadiah lived in a very difficult situation. He was loyal to the king, and his position as steward required that he carry out the king's will in all things. The problem was that Jezebel hated the people of God and made it her priority to destroy the Lord's prophets at every opportunity. Obadiah's first loyalty was to the Lord, and he could not comply with the queen's wishes; in fact, he was compelled to fight against her determination to murder the prophets.

So Obadiah took a terrible risk by hiding one hundred prophets in caves, protecting them from Jezebel's murderous hatred. Had he been caught, the queen would have put him to death without hesitation, and the king would have viewed his actions as open treachery. His bravery on that occasion called for secrecy, but the Lord next called him to act courageously and openly on His behalf. If Obadiah had given in to his fears, he might have refused to obey God openly, and that would have been like a public denial of the Lord. He would in effect have been saying that he feared the king's wrath more than he trusted God's sovereignty.

Fear causes us to distrust God's loving hand of provision and protection. It grows when we focus on the thing that frightens us, rather than on the God who protects us. This is the reason that the Lord commands His people to be courageous, because faith requires courage—believing that God will protect His people, and acting on that belief. The Lord's words to Joshua apply to us as well: "Have I not commanded you? Be strong and of good courage; do not be afraid, nor be dismayed, for the LORD your God is with you wherever you go" (Joshua 1:9).

⌁ DIGGING DEEPER ⌁

5. *What sort of dangers and conflicts would Obadiah have faced as a God-fearing man working in Ahab's household?*

6. *From a human perspective, why was Obadiah likely chosen to be the king's steward? From God's perspective, why was he given that responsibility?*

7. *How did fear affect Obadiah's view of God? What finally gave him the courage to take an open stand for the Lord? How can the Lord's promises give you courage this week?*

8.   When have you obeyed the Lord in secret? When have you been rewarded openly by Him? What has He done in your life that reassures you that you belong to Him?

↤ Taking It Personally ↦

9.   What work has the Lord given you to do? Are you doing it with all your might, or do you sometimes have a "good enough" attitude?

10. Is the Lord calling you to be courageous in some area of life? What is it that requires courage? How can Obadiah's example help you to be more courageous?

~ 9 ~
THE STARVING WIDOW

⌁ CHARACTER'S BACKGROUND ⌁

The people of Elijah's day were dependent upon farming. There were no supermarkets where one could purchase food; most people lived on what they were able to grow for themselves. If there was no rain, hunger and starvation were real possibilities. Because farming was hard work, it was for the most part a man's work. A woman and her children depended heavily upon the man of the house to provide food and shelter. A widow without family would almost certainly starve to death under normal circumstances, and especially in the midst of the severe drought that took place during Elijah's lifetime.

As it happened, while Elijah was being fed by ravens there was such a widow living in the city of Zarephath. This woman had a young son, and she was very poor—but what particularly distinguished her from her neighbors was not her financial situation but her faith. This woman lived between Tyre and Sidon, which was the heartland of Baal worship at the time. Indeed, her king was Jezebel's father, a man who hated the people of God as much as his wicked daughter did. Yet here was this woman, in the midst of the pagans, worshiping Israel's God!

One might expect that the Lord would bless such a faithful and courageous woman with great wealth and perfect health, but such was not the case. This woman was so poor that she was getting ready to eat her last meal at the moment when Elijah arrived, and her son's health was soon to deteriorate and end in sudden death. This woman, it turns out, was actually very rich, but her wealth was not in gold—it was in a powerful faith and obedience to the King of kings.

The Lord did honor that great faith, and He did so not by showering wealth upon the poor widow, but by giving her yet more faith. Her great faith and obedience provide an example for us today.

GOD SENDS ELIJAH TO THE HEATHEN: *Elijah has been living by the Brook Cherith for some time, but now the Lord sends him off to the heart of Baal worship.*

7. AFTER A WHILE: Elijah had been living by the Brook Cherith for an unspecified amount of time, being fed by ravens as we saw in Study 4. Elijah was depending upon the brook for water, yet the Lord allowed it eventually to dry up. There is an old saying that, when the Lord closes a door, He opens a window—and this passage provides an excellent example of that principle. The Lord permitted the brook to dry up because He had another job for Elijah in another location.

9. ZAREPHATH: A town on the Mediterranean coast about midway between Tyre and Sidon. (See the map in the Introduction.) This territory was ruled over by Jezebel's father, who was also the high priest of Baal at the time. This is a significant location, since the widow was living in the very heart of Baal worship—yet she was faithful to the God of Israel.

I HAVE COMMANDED A WIDOW THERE: This suggests that the widow was a follower of God, obedient to His commands. Like Obadiah, she was obedient to the Lord at the risk of grave danger to herself. If Jezebel did not hesitate to murder the Lord's prophets in Israel, how much more would her father have slaughtered any of God's people in Sidon! Her faith in the Lord is even more remarkable, since she was not a Jew and did not live in Israel.

THREE TESTS: *The Lord asks the woman to obey Him on faith, even though her actions could prove costly—and potentially lead to starvation. Yet she obeys anyway.*

10. GATHERING STICKS: This underscores the widow's dire poverty. She did not even have the materials on hand to build a fire, never mind enough food to cook a meal.

BRING ME A LITTLE WATER: Elijah's first request might be viewed as a small test to discern whether or not this was the woman to whom God had sent him. The drought was severe, and even a cup of water would have been highly valued, yet this widow left off her task of gathering sticks to go get some for a thirsty stranger. The widow did not know it yet, but she was serving God's anointed prophet, and her reward would be great.

11. BRING ME A MORSEL OF BREAD: Elijah's second request was more severe than it might seem. He was asking the widow to part with her last meal. In short, Elijah was asking her to put her hope of being provided for completely in the Lord's hands.

12. As the Lord your God lives: The widow here acknowledged that she served the living God. Such words were bold in the gate of a city that was devoted to Baal worship, yet she did not try to hide the fact that she did not serve false gods.

That we may eat it, and die: The widow was gathering sticks with which to cook the last meal for herself and her son. She had nothing else, and no prospect of getting anything else, and the future (as far as she could discern) held only death by starvation for them both. Her calm demeanor in this situation was striking. She did not engage in any dramatics; neither did she pour out complaints to God's prophet. In fact, she did not even mention her urgent need at Elijah's first request for water, but only when he went on to request food. Her actions and attitude demonstrate that she held a quiet faith in God, and she knew that her future (and her son's future) was in His hands.

13. Do not fear: Once again we see the importance of courage in the life of faith. Elijah was about to ask the woman to do something that would require great faith, and he knew that fear would prompt the woman to refuse—and if she refused, she would lose an opportunity to see the Lord's miraculous provision for her family. But if she chose to act with courage, obeying the Lord's commands and leaving the consequences in His hands, then her obedience would bring great reward, and her faith would grow even stronger.

Make me a small cake from it first: This request was the most difficult of all to fulfill. Elijah wanted the widow to take what little flour she had—itself barely enough to feed herself and her son—and to use a portion of it first to make a cake for him. We can see an increasing difficulty in the three requests of Elijah: first, "bring me some water"; second, "bring me some food"; third, "make my food first, before you feed your starving family." The Lord was emptying this woman of all she could hope in and leaving her with nothing except her faith in God. But the Lord already knew that her faith was strong enough before He asked this of her, for He never tests us beyond our abilities to pass the test (1 Corinthians 10:13).

15. She . . . did according to the word of Elijah: This woman was not an Israelite, and did not have the rich heritage and teaching of God's Law that was freely available in Israel—yet she willingly obeyed the prophet's instructions, even at great cost to herself, while the people of Israel willfully disobeyed the prophets and the God who had sent them.

16. The bin of flour was not used up: God had miraculously provided manna for His people during their exodus from Egypt, feeding them but not the surrounding nations. Now the tables were turned, as He miraculously provided food each morning for this foreign widow, while leaving Israel in famine.

Death and Resurrection: *Sometime later, the widow's son dies, and she turns to the prophet of God for help. The Lord then strengthens her faith by raising her son back to life.*

17. NO BREATH LEFT IN HIM: In other words, the boy died.

18. BRING MY SIN TO REMEMBRANCE: The widow in her grief assumed that her son had died in some sort of divine retribution for her own sins. This is a common response of human nature in times of great sorrow, but it is not an accurate view of God. She was correct in recognizing that her son's life was entirely in God's hands, but not in thinking her son died because of her own sins.

19. THE UPPER ROOM WHERE HE WAS STAYING: Elijah occupied a small room on the rooftop of the house, accessible only from outside. This afforded him his own private quarters, and also avoided even the appearance of any inappropriate relationship with the widow.

20. HAVE YOU ALSO BROUGHT TRAGEDY ON THE WIDOW:. We can certainly understand that Elijah considered the boy's death a great tragedy. The widow was mystified that Elijah would save her boy's life during the famine only to take it now, and Elijah was unable to explain what God was doing.

BY KILLING HER SON: Elijah also recognized that all life is in the hands of God, and that it was God Himself who had allowed this boy to die. His deep grief also indicates how much he cared about the widow and her son.

21. HE STRETCHED HIMSELF OUT ON THE CHILD THREE TIMES: Elijah was not performing mouth-to-mouth resuscitation here, because the boy was not unconscious; he was dead. Why Elijah did this is not clear, but what is clear is that Elijah was fervently praying for the boy.

22. THE LORD HEARD THE VOICE OF ELIJAH: The Lord always hears the cries of His children, and He is always faithful to respond. There are times, however, when He waits for us to ask before He sends an answer. Here the Lord showed that the power to raise the boy was found not in Elijah but rather in God, the author of life.

23. YOUR SON LIVES: This is the first recorded instance of resurrection in the Bible.

24. BY THIS I KNOW THAT YOU ARE A MAN OF GOD: The widow had already placed her faith in God's Word simply by obeying what He asked her to do with her last remnants of food. But here she had seen a dramatic demonstration of God's power that surpassed even the miraculous renewal of food each day, for only God can defeat the powers of death. It is important to recognize, however, that her faith and obedience preceded this great miracle; she obeyed the Lord on faith, and He strengthened that faith with a clear demonstration of His great power and love. The Jews in Jesus' day, by contrast, demanded a sign, but they were denied because they had already refused to place their faith and trust in God (Luke 11:29–32).

↭ First Impressions ↭

1. *Why did God send Elijah to live with the widow in Zarephath? What did He want to accomplish for the widow? For the people of Zarephath?*

2. *Why did Elijah ask the woman for water? for food? Why did he insist that she make food for him before making it for herself and her son?*

3. *Why did the woman honor Elijah's requests, even though he was a complete stranger to her? What did her actions reveal about her faith in God?*

4. *If you had been in the widow's place, how would you have reacted when your son died? when Elijah asked you for his body? when he was resurrected?*

∼ Some Key Principles ∼

The Lord sometimes requires obedience before He sends His blessing.

The widow in this passage feared God and served Him alone, even though she lived in a land that was openly hostile to the things of God. It was no coincidence that the Lord sent His prophet Elijah to her, because He intended to pour out His blessings upon her, providing her with food and water at a time when the rest of the world was starving. But before He demonstrated His power to her, He required that she demonstrate her faith to the world around her.

When we speak of the Lord "testing our faith," we should understand that it is not a test like the ones we were given in school, intended to find out how much faith we have; the Lord already knows our hearts, and He discerns the strength of our faith. His tests are designed to demonstrate outwardly the extent of our faith, as a testimony to the world that God's children trust Him fully; and they also are intended to strengthen our faith even further. The widow's faith was strengthened and deepened when she obeyed the Lord's commands, and she also testified to the Baal-centered world around her that the God of Israel is the only true God.

God desires deeply to send blessing upon blessing into the lives of His children, but there are times when we cannot fully receive those blessings unless we first obey His Word. The important thing to remember in this regard is that the Lord already knows our limits, and He has promised that He will never send us a test or a trial that is too great for us to bear: "No temptation has overtaken you except such as is common to man; but God is faithful, who will not allow you to be tempted beyond what you are able, but with the temptation will also make the way of escape, that you may be able to bear it" (1 Corinthians 10:13).

All life is from God.

The death of the young boy in this passage was a terrific blow to the widow, both because of the terrible grief over losing her son and also because, in human terms, he represented her hope for the future; she needed him to grow to manhood and look after her in old age, since her husband was already dead. Yet even in her devastating grief, she turned to the Lord for help, by way of His prophet Elijah. She recognized that God is the author of all life, and that He alone has authority over death—and resurrection.

There are no recorded instances of someone being brought back from the dead prior to this passage in Scripture; yet the widow was quick to give her dead son into Elijah's hands the moment he asked. Canaanite myths of that time claimed that Baal could restore life to the dead, but needless to say, such a thing had never happened. By putting her dead son's body into Elijah's hands, the widow was demonstrating her faith that God had the power that all false gods lacked: the power to restore her son to life.

The Scriptures are emphatic on this point, from the first chapter of Genesis to the final chapter of Revelation: God is the author and sustainer of all life. He spoke life into existence at creation (Genesis 1), and the river of life flows from His throne in eternity (Revelation 22). Jesus said, "I am the bread of life" (John 6:48); "I am the resurrection and the life. He who believes in Me, though he may die, he shall live" (John 11:25); and "I am the way, the truth, and the life. No one comes to the Father except through Me" (John 14:6). Life is a gift given directly from the hand of God, and He alone has authority over life and death.

Obey God's Word, and leave the consequences in His hands.

The Lord asked a starving widow to feed a complete stranger, even as she was gathering twigs to cook her last small bit of flour before facing utter starvation. This was a very costly step of faith on her part, since she was responsible not only for her own food but also for feeding her son. As a widow in an agrarian culture, she had no easy way of providing food for her family, and no husband who could provide an income. She was on the point of starvation, and faced the prospect of watching her son die with her. Yet the Lord asked her to share what little she had left with a stranger (v. 9), and she obeyed.

At that point, the widow was demonstrating a deep faith in the character and power of the Lord. She was willing to do what He asked, even though it might potentially mean the death of her entire family, but she was willing to obey God's commands and leave the future in His hands. This is the essence of faith, to obey God's Word simply because He is our Lord, even when there might be some costly consequences from such obedience. Our faith is based upon His faithfulness, and we rest in the assurance that He will work out the future to His glory and our blessing.

The widow was not disappointed, and neither will we be when we follow her example. The Lord was not hampered by the drought, and He was fully able to provide her with food and oil for as long as needed. He is not hampered by any circumstances in our lives today either, and He is still faithful to provide for His children's needs. Our job is not to worry about the future, but to obey God's Word today; He will take care of whatever follows from our obedience.

⤳ Digging Deeper ⤢

5. How did this woman's faith contrast with the faith of most Israelites at the time? What spiritual benefits did Israel enjoy that the woman did not have? What blessings did she gain that Israel lacked?

6. How strong was the widow's faith in the Lord when she first met Elijah? What did the Lord do to make it even stronger? How had her faith grown by the end of this passage?

7.   Was the woman wrong to have such an emotional response to her son's death? How do you see her faith even in the way she reacts to this event?

8.   When have you obeyed God's Word, even though you were uncertain what consequences it might bring? How did that obedience strengthen your faith?

9. How well are you trusting the Lord's authority over life and death? Do you struggle with fears regarding your mortality? Do you trust Him with the lives of your loved ones?

10. Is the Lord calling you to costly obedience today? What consequences do you fear? How will you overcome your fear and leave those consequences in His hands?

SECTION 3:

THEMES

In This Section:

~ 10 ~
THE SIN OF SYNCRETISM

ᴧ THEMATIC BACKGROUND ᴧ

Syncretism is the practice of combining the teachings of the world with the teachings of Scripture. For example, the world teaches that the human race evolved from lower life forms over many millions of years, while the Bible teaches that God created the entire universe from nothing in six days. If we attempt to reconcile these opposing views, altering the Word of God in order to accommodate the teachings of the world, we commit the sin of syncretism.

Jeroboam committed this sin, as we saw in Study 2, when he created his own new religious system. He crafted two golden calves and encouraged Israel to pray to them, and he instituted his own order of priests to make sacrifices to the Lord *and* to the idols. He did not abolish worship of God in Israel; he merely redesigned it to fit his own needs. This is the sin of syncretism.

Syncretism is motivated by a person's desire to live life his own way, to worship God on his own terms. It may not be a wholesale rejection of God's Word—just parts of it that don't fit one's agenda. It might involve ignoring some principles, and it might include inventing new principles, but it ultimately involves rewriting God's Word in order to serve oneself. And this is a form of idolatry.

ᴧ READING 1 KINGS 14:1–18 ᴧ

JEROBOAM'S SON: *Shortly after the events from Study 2, King Jeroboam's son becomes gravely ill. In this moment of crisis, Jeroboam turns to God rather than his idols.*

1. AT THAT TIME: This passage takes place during the reign of Jeroboam, just after the events in Study 2.

ABIJAH: The name means "my father is the Lord," and it suggests that Jeroboam wanted to be seen as a worshiper of the God of Israel. He may even have considered himself as such, but the Lord viewed his syncretistic practices as pure idolatry. Mixing paganism with Christianity is not being cultured; it is being unfaithful to God's Word.

2. DISGUISE YOURSELF: Jeroboam evidently wanted to deceive both the prophet of God and the people of Israel. This suggests that he was unwilling to be seen by the people consulting a prophet of God, rather than one of the priests whom he had appointed. (See Study 2 for further information.) After all, he had invented a new religious system for the people of Israel, telling them that they could incorporate idolatry into their worship practices and still please God. Yet his consulting Ahijah indicates that he knew his own syncretistic religion to be worthless; in a time of crisis, he turned back to obedience to the Lord.

AHIJAH THE PROPHET: Ahijah had met Jeroboam and predicted that the Lord would give him the ten northern tribes (1 Kings 11:29–39). He had also told Jeroboam that the Lord would establish his throne if he obeyed God's commands. Ahijah's prophecies had come to pass, demonstrating that he was a true man of God and not a false prophet.

3. TEN LOAVES: This gift would have been suitable for a common laborer, but not for a king. Jeroboam was hoping to deceive the prophet completely about his wife's identity, which demonstrates how deeply confused his thinking was. On one hand, he recognized that Ahijah was a prophet of God, capable of predicting future events as revealed by the Lord; on the other hand, he thought that he could hide his wife's identity from such a man by the ruse of a simple disguise.

THE BLIND SEER: *Ahijah is blind, but he doesn't need physical eyes to see the truth. The Lord gives him true spiritual sight, which cannot be deceived by silly disguises.*

4. AHIJAH COULD NOT SEE: The irony here is that the disguise was completely wasted, since Ahijah couldn't see anyway. But the loss of his physical sight had no bearing upon his spiritual sight.

5. HERE IS THE WIFE OF JEROBOAM: It is conceivable that the woman's disguise might have deceived Ahijah in his blindness, just as Isaac was deceived by Jacob's disguise (Genesis 27), but God's eyes are never blinded. The Lord sees all things, and He sees more clearly and accurately than any human eyes can. Just as He saw Ahab in Naboth's vineyard (1 Kings 21:18), so here He was watching as Jeroboam's wife traveled on her deceitful errand. Notice that His eyes were also on Jeroboam's sick son.

6. COME IN, WIFE OF JEROBOAM: Imagine how startled Jeroboam's wife must have been when she heard these words! Yet the greeting also served to let her know that Ahijah's message was from the Lord.

PRETEND TO BE ANOTHER PERSON: Jeroboam had long been doing this very thing, pretending to serve the God of Israel when in fact he was pursuing false gods. A person may deceive himself into thinking that he is following the Word of God while actually pursuing his own way, but God is not mocked.

GOD'S COMING JUDGMENT: *The Lord prophesies through Ahijah that Jeroboam's son will die. What's worse, his entire house will be put to death because of his syncretism.*

7. I EXALTED YOU: Jeroboam was not born into a royal household, and he had no right (in earthly terms) to become king. But the Lord had lifted him up and given him responsibility for His people of Israel. The king's role was to lead God's people into obedience to His commands, leading by example—but Jeroboam had done just the opposite, leading Israel away from God by incorporating idolatry into Israel's proper worship practices.

8. TORE THE KINGDOM AWAY FROM THE HOUSE OF DAVID: David had been a man after God's own heart, and the Lord had established his throne forever. Yet He had been willing to tear away the kingdom from David's descendants when Solomon did not remain faithful to the whole Word of God. How much more so, then, would the Lord be willing to tear it away from Jeroboam, who had not walked in His ways!

9. ALL WHO WERE BEFORE YOU: Solomon had followed the Lord with a divided heart, as we saw in Study 1, but Jeroboam's sin was even more immoral than Solomon's. Jeroboam had deliberately introduced pagan practices in Israel, willfully leading the nation away from the Lord's commands in order to strengthen his own position of power.

CAST ME BEHIND YOUR BACK: This is a powerful picture of the sin of syncretism. A person effectively thrusts God behind his back when he determines to add to and delete from the Word of God, making himself the leader and God the follower—or attempting to do so. This is essentially the same sin committed by Lucifer, who sought to make himself equal with God (Isaiah 14:12–14).

10. AS ONE TAKES AWAY REFUSE: The Lord was going to remove Jeroboam and his household from Israel as though He were throwing out the garbage. This is a powerful statement on how God views man's syncretistic practices. He commands obedience to His Word as it is written, and any deviation from that is like smelly rubbish.

11. DOGS SHALL EAT WHOEVER BELONGS TO JEROBOAM: As we saw with Jezebel, it was a sign of being cursed by God if one died and lay unburied. The Lord's wrath against Jeroboam was severe for his syncretism, yet He had warned His people that this very fate would befall them if they adulterated their worship with pagan practices (Deuteronomy 28:26).

13. WHO SHALL COME TO THE GRAVE: That is, this was the only son of Jeroboam who would receive the honor of a proper burial.

SOMETHING GOOD TOWARD THE LORD: We are not told what the Lord saw in Abijah's character, but He did find something in the young man that pleased Him. The Lord's eyes are always on His children, not in hopes of searching out evil and sin, but in order to show Himself faithful and to bring blessing (2 Chronicles 16:9).

15. HE WILL UPROOT ISRAEL FROM THIS GOOD LAND: The Lord was prophesying that He would eventually send the nation of Israel into captivity for her sins of idolatry, which did occur nearly one hundred years later (2 Kings 17:22–23). Yet this was not a surprise to the Israelites, for the Lord had warned them that He would do this if they chased after foreign gods (Deuteronomy 28:63–64).

16. HE WILL GIVE ISRAEL UP: That is, the Lord would give them into the hands of their enemies. Israel's idolatry eventually led them into captivity, yet the Lord never abandoned them. He does send discipline into the lives of His children, but He will never cast us away completely.

⌁ First Impressions ⌁

1. *Why did Jeroboam send his wife to Ahijah instead of to one of the priests he had appointed? (See Study 2.) What does this reveal about his syncretistic beliefs?*

2. *Why did Jeroboam have his wife wear a disguise? What did he hope to accomplish? What does this reveal about his views of God?*

3.   Why did the Lord allow Jeroboam's son to die? to be buried? What does it mean that there was "something good toward the LORD" in him (v. 13)?

4.   How did Jeroboam's sin differ from the sins of Solomon? How were they similar? In what ways did Solomon's sins open the door for the sin of Jeroboam?

᜔ Some Key Principles ᜔

Syncretism is a form of idolatry.

Syncretism refers to the act of mixing together elements from different religions to create a sort of hybrid religious system. The process can refer to intermingling diverse religious practices, or it can refer to those who attempt to reconcile opposing viewpoints. Jeroboam committed the sin of syncretism when he attempted to mingle pagan idolatry together with God's commanded worship. It is easy to see the idolatry of Jeroboam's acts, since he literally created two golden calves for the people to worship.

But syncretism is still idolatry even when it doesn't involve golden calves. The basic motivation behind syncretism is rebellion against God's Word. A person decides that he wants to worship God in his own way, and rejects certain aspects of Scripture in favor of his own ideas or practices. This is the idolatry of self, making oneself to be equal with God and pushing God into the background, just as Jeroboam did. The world continually encourages syncretism for the simple reason that it hates the teachings of Christ and does everything in its power to move believers away from God's Word. The claim that the gospel must be made "relevant" to our culture is used as an excuse by many to ignore some scriptural principles and add in principles that are not scriptural—but such attempts are syncretistic, attempting to mix the teachings of the world into the doctrines of God's Word.

The Bible is the final authority on how to approach God, and no man has the privilege of rewriting Scripture to fit his own desires or to fit into the culture of the world around him. When cultural teachings and practices go against the teachings of the Bible, then we are called to choose between the two—but not to attempt some compromise incorporating elements of both. Elijah confronted the people of Israel at Mount Carmel on this very issue, calling them to choose once and for all to serve God, and to serve Him in His way, not their own way. Anything else is idolatry.

Even non-believers call on God in times of trouble.

Jeroboam is a fascinating case study about how those who reject God's authority still call on Him in times of trouble. Jeroboam made no secret of his disdain for God and His Word. He instituted his own priesthood, he rejected the traditional Jewish holidays and replaced them with his own, and he even built altars to gods whom he invented. In short, Jeroboam rejected God and replaced Him with his own religion. But when Jeroboam's hand was withered, he immediately asked the prophet to pray for him (1 Kings 13:6). And again, when his son fell ill, he sent his wife to the prophet. Jeroboam's hypocrisy is so obvious it's startling, and it crystallizes the dilemma of those who reject God. On the one hand, Jeroboam invented his own religion and rejected the Lord of the universe. But on the other hand, his new religion was powerless to heal him or save his son. It is ironic when circumstances force the non-believer to outwardly call on God for help.

This kind of plea for help does not reflect a genuine desire to have a relationship with God. For example, when God did heal Jeroboam's hand, it did not result in Jeroboam's repentance. It is naïve to think that, had God also healed his son, Jeroboam would have submitted his life to God's authority. Conversion comes when a person humbles himself and realizes that God is good and holy, while sinners are deserving of judgment. When a sinner cries to God for forgiveness, it is granted. When a non-believer cries to God in the face of a trial, God may or may not answer, as these cries are not indicative of true repentance.

The ultimate trial, of course, is death. When non-believers stand before God for judgment, there will be many who, like Jeroboam, will call out to the Lord for help. Jesus said that in death there will be many who will say to Him, "Lord, Lord," but He will cast them away, because He never really knew them (Matthew 7:22–23).

God's discipline is for our good.

The people of Israel rebelled against the Lord, rejecting His commands and insisting upon walking in their own ways. In fact, the nation's history is riddled with such rebellion, from the time that the Israelites left Egypt right through to the time that the Lord sent them into captivity. The Lord continually showed Himself faithful and loving to His people—and they continually showed themselves to be rebellious, ever insisting upon living their lives as they saw fit.

This tendency, however, is not unique to the nation of Israel. On the contrary, it is common to all mankind. We are all descendants of Adam, and we all possess Adam's fallen and rebellious nature. The Lord rebuked and disciplined Israel repeatedly throughout the nation's history, and He will do the same to His children today. But we must remember that His discipline is as much a part of His loving faithfulness as is His blessing; all that He does in the lives of believers is designed for our benefit, intended to make us into the image of His Son, Jesus.

The Lord will never abandon His children. The day of judgment is indeed coming, and there will be many who will be cast out of God's presence—but those who are redeemed through the blood of Christ shall never be cast out. We may suffer hardship and discipline, for, as stated above, the Lord does discipline those whom He loves (Hebrews 12:5–6), but no Christian needs to fear that God will abandon him. "The LORD . . . will not leave you nor forsake you" (Deuteronomy 31:8).

⌁ DIGGING DEEPER ⌁

5. Define syncretism in your own words. Why is it a sinful practice? Why does God view it as stinking garbage (v. 10)?

6. In what ways is syncretism a form of idolatry? What is idolatrous about it? What motivates a person to commit syncretism?

7. What is the difference between God's discipline and God's judgment? What is God's purpose when He sends discipline into our lives?

8. Give some examples of syncretism that have crept into Christian teachings today. What does the Bible say about each?

↬ TAKING IT PERSONALLY ↫

9. How do we know that Christians will never face judgment? Give evidence from the Scriptures.

10. Have you allowed syncretism into your relationship with God? What will you do to remove worldly elements from your worship?

~ II ~
BE FAITHFUL TO GOD'S WORD

1 KINGS 22

~ THEMATIC BACKGROUND ~

The book of 1 Kings is filled with the stories of numerous kings and various prophets, but one trend runs throughout them all: the kings of Israel rejected the Word of God, while the prophets of God spoke the truth to them boldly. In every case, those who rejected God's truth came to destruction, while the words of the prophets have always proven true. In this study, we will finally see the words of Elijah and others come to reality in the life of Ahab, and we will see God's hand of judgment come down on that wicked king.

We will also meet Jehoshaphat, a king of Judah who actually fears the Lord and seeks to do His will. We will find him, of all places, in the court of Ahab, as the two kings—polar opposites in their approach to God's Word—make plans to go into war together. One might well ask what Jehoshaphat was doing there in the first place, but the answer is another theme that has run throughout these studies: Jehoshaphat had allied himself with the wicked family of Ahab through an ungodly marriage, uniting his son to Ahab's daughter. The results of this unequal yoking were consistent with all the others that we've seen in these passages.

This study will demonstrate very clearly how the ungodly hate truth, and the lengths to which people will go to avoid the truth and replace it with lies—lies that make them happy, even when they know they're lies. This is the inevitable result for anyone who rejects the Word of God; it is the wise person who remains faithful to God's Word.

~ READING 1 KINGS 22:1–38 ~

MAKING PLANS FOR WAR: *Jehoshaphat, king of Judah, joins Ahab in Israel, and the two consider making war against Syria once again.*

1. THREE YEARS PASSED: Ben-Hadad, the king of Syria, had made war against Israel, and the Lord had given His people a great victory—but Ahab had spared his life against the Lord's command, making a peace treaty with him instead. (See 1 Kings 20 for the full account.)

2. JEHOSHAPHAT: The fourth king of Judah. His son Jehoram married Ahab's daughter Athaliah (2 Kings 8:16–18), an alliance that would prove harmful for Jehoshaphat and calamitous for Jehoram. Jehoshaphat felt compelled by this relationship to associate himself with Ahab, while Ahab's daughter would eventually lead Jehoram into the idolatrous ways of Israel.

THE KING OF ISRAEL: That is, Ahab.

3. RAMOTH IN GILEAD: See the map in the Introduction. Ben-Hadad had promised to return to Ahab all the Israelite cities that Syria had taken away, but he evidently had not fulfilled that promise.

SEEKING GOD'S WILL: *Jehoshaphat does not want to make plans without first asking what the Lord desires. This raises a problem, since only one king serves the Lord.*

5. PLEASE INQUIRE FOR THE WORD OF THE LORD: Jehoshaphat set an example to Ahab by insisting that they seek the Lord's counsel before going into battle. It seems likely that Ahab would have charged forward without the Lord's guidance if Jehoshaphat had not insisted.

6. GATHERED THE PROPHETS TOGETHER: These were not true prophets of the Lord, but false prophets whom Ahab had gathered around him. They worshiped the golden calves set up by Jeroboam, so their words were obviously not from God.

7. A PROPHET OF THE LORD: Jehoshaphat recognized that these men were not true prophets, and insisted once again that they consult a man whose words would be from God.

8. BUT I HATE HIM: One can almost picture Ahab stamping his foot and pouting as he said these words. Once again we see his childish behavior, demanding his own way. The prophet Micaiah had the courage to speak the truth to Ahab, but Ahab was less interested in hearing the truth than in hearing words that pleased him.

LET NOT THE KING SAY SUCH THINGS: Jehoshaphat rebuked Ahab for his wicked attitude, because he was placing his own desires above the true word of God spoken by His prophet. The true prophet of God will speak God's Word, whether it brings a message of encouragement or judgment, but the false prophet of the world will design his message to please his hearers.

9. BRING MICAIAH ... QUICKLY: It appears that Ahab was growing impatient at this point. He certainly didn't want to be confronted by Micaiah, for fear that the prophet would say things that displeased him, but he also wanted to do what Jehoshaphat asked, because he wanted to go to battle. He had already convinced himself that his plan was right, and was impatient to get on with it. Ahab was consistently both immature and impetuous.

The False Prophets Speak: *Ahab brings in four hundred of his own handpicked prophets, men who could be counted on to say "the right things"—whether or not they were right.*

10. AT A THRESHING FLOOR: The threshing floor was a hard-packed space in the open air where wheat and other grains were beaten out. The threshing separated the edible portion from the inedible chaff. Threshing floors were common sites for meetings of royal courts in Canaan at the time, but threshing is also used in Scripture to speak of God's winnowing process, in which He separates the wheat from the chaff, the godly from the fleshly. It was an appropriate setting for this important meeting, as God was about to separate the truth from lies, the godly from the ungodly.

11. ZEDEKIAH . . . HAD MADE HORNS OF IRON FOR HIMSELF: Zedekiah was evidently the spokesman for the four hundred false prophets. He used visual aids in his presentation to the kings, which undoubtedly made his message seem more convincing and powerful. But the Lord's truth is frequently couched in very humble terms, while the messages of the world are often far more entertaining and compelling to the flesh.

THUS SAYS THE LORD: By speaking these words, Zedekiah was claiming that his message was a direct revelation from God. Anyone who made this claim falsely was to be put to death, and the test of validity was whether or not the prophesied events came to pass (Deuteronomy 18:20–22).

12. ALL THE PROPHETS PROPHESIED SO: The false prophets were unanimous in their encouragement. Ahab had surrounded himself with people who would tell him exactly what he wanted to hear, and would couch it in religious language. They did not disappoint. Nothing could ruin Ahab's plan but for a real prophet to show up and contradict the false prophecies.

God's Prophet Speaks: *Under pressure from Jehoshaphat, Ahab finally sends for Micaiah, a prophet of the Lord.*

13. NOW LISTEN: One can picture this messenger whispering in Micaiah's ear, offering him some worldly wisdom. "Don't rock the boat," he essentially said. "Everyone else is in agreement on this; do yourself a favor—do *everyone* a favor—and just go along with it."

14. THAT I WILL SPEAK: The prophet of God always speaks the truth, whether or not it will sit comfortably with those who hear it.

15. GO AND PROSPER: Micaiah was not actually delivering the Lord's message at this point, but was using sarcasm to underscore the fact that Ahab's prophets were only saying what he wanted to hear. Elijah also used sarcasm and irony on Carmel to accentuate the absolute powerlessness of false gods (1 Kings 18:27).

16. TELL ME NOTHING BUT THE TRUTH: It is significant that Ahab made this demand. It demonstrated that he recognized Micaiah's sarcasm, understanding that it was not the word of the Lord; and it also revealed that, in his heart, Ahab knew that his own wise men were false prophets.

17. SHEEP THAT HAVE NO SHEPHERD: Jesus described Himself as the "good shepherd" (John 10:11), stating that the good shepherd is willing to lay down his life for the sheep. Ahab, by contrast, was willing to sacrifice the lives of others for his own fleshly desires. It is no coincidence that David had been a shepherd before becoming king, and he led the nation the way God intended. The fact is that Israel had not had a good shepherd from the time that Ahab took power. Micaiah's prophecy indicated that Ahab would be killed in battle.

19. HEAR THE WORD OF THE LORD: Micaiah was claiming that his words were a direct revelation from God, just as Zedekiah had claimed. The two prophecies, however, were mutually exclusive—they could not both be true. The final test would be to see which prophecy came true; the prophecy that did not come to pass was not a word from the Lord, and the one who spoke that prophecy was a false prophet whose words were to be completely discredited.

A LYING SPIRIT: *The Lord had sent an evil spirit to influence the false prophets in order to urge Ahab into battle.*

I SAW THE LORD: Micaiah evidently had a vision from the Lord. Other prophets recorded such visions, including Isaiah (Isaiah 6) and the apostle John (Revelation 1:9; 4:1).

20. WHO WILL PERSUADE AHAB: Many prophetic visions describe conversations between God and angelic beings within His heavenly court. Job, for example, described such a conversation involving Satan, who was permitted to test God's faithful servant Job (Job 1–2).

22. A LYING SPIRIT: This creature who spoke these words was a demonic spirit, because good angels do not lie. This spirit was loyal to the devil, but the devil is not an independent being; he is subject to the authority and power of God, and must come and go from His presence at His command. The devil is also the father of lies, and has been a murderer from the beginning of creation (Genesis 3; John 8:44).

Go out and do so: Here we see that evil spirits are entirely subject to the will and commands of God—yet the Lord also permits them to commit wickedness. In this way, the Lord uses all things, even the wickedness of Satan, to further His own plans. Nothing can thwart God's sovereignty, not even the enemy of mankind. We must also remember, however, that those who disobey God's Word will be accountable for their disobedience, just as Ahab was about to be brought to account for his wickedness.

23. The Lord has put a lying spirit: The Lord "put" the lying spirit in the mouths of the false prophets in the sense that He permitted demons to mislead them. God is not the author of evil, however, and He never lies—nor does He ever encourage His creatures to speak lies. This is an example of how God permits evil, using it to further His own plans—but it does not condone the evil behavior in the process.

these prophets of yours: The false prophets were prophets of Ahab, not prophets of God. They spoke the words that the king wanted to hear without regard to the Lord's truth. The world today is filled with such false prophets, who preach tantalizing doctrines that are entirely contrary to the Word of God.

24. struck Micaiah on the cheek: The world's prophets go beyond ignoring the Word of God—they actually hate it, and they hate those who preach it, often lashing out at the prophet. Jesus received similar treatment from the chief priests (Mark 14:65).

27. Put this fellow in prison: The Lord does permit His servants to suffer for His Word, even as He suffered on the cross. Ahab's foolishness was on clear display here. He mistakenly thought that if he jailed the prophet, God would let him live. Simply put, Ahab was trying to manipulate the Lord.

28. If you ever return in peace ... Take heed: Once again, Micaiah reiterated the test for all prophets. If just one prophecy does not come to pass or is in contradiction to the written Word of God, that person is not speaking God's message.

Ahab's Last Stand: *Ahab disregards the Lord's dire warnings and goes off to battle, thinking he can outsmart God by changing his clothes.*

30. I will disguise myself: This suggests that Ahab feared that Micaiah's prophecy would come to pass. Kings generally wore royal robes into battle so that their army would see them leading the charge. This also made them an easy target for the enemy, since their clothes made them stand out in the heat of battle. Ahab may also have been deliberately treacherous to Jehoshaphat in this plan, since Jehoshaphat would stand out all the more conspicuously if he was the only king in royal attire. It is surprising that Jehoshaphat went along with the plan, and suggests a lack of wisdom on his part in allying himself with Ahab in this battle, especially after the Lord's prophet had foretold disaster.

31. THE KING OF SYRIA: This was Ben-Hadad, whom Ahab had allowed to live after Israel had defeated the Syrian army. The Lord had prophesied that Ahab would give his life in exchange for Ben-Hadad (1 Kings 20:42), and here the divine prediction was fulfilled.

34. A CERTAIN MAN DREW A BOW AT RANDOM: Ahab thought he could outsmart the sovereign God by simply disguising himself, much as Jeroboam tried to do. (See Study 10.) But God's purposes cannot be thwarted, and His promises always come true. The Lord used an unnamed soldier who shot an arrow at random, and He guided that arrow into a tiny chink in Ahab's armor. This would be perceived by the world as a random event, a striking coincidence, but it was actually God's deliberate hand intervening to work a miracle.

35. THE KING WAS PROPPED UP IN HIS CHARIOT: If the army of Israel saw their king fall in battle, they would turn and flee, so Ahab's servants propped him up to appear as though he were still fighting. In reality, he had already died.

38. THE DOGS LICKED UP HIS BLOOD: This was just what Elijah had prophesied (1 Kings 21:19).

WHILE THE HARLOTS BATHED: Ahab had prostituted himself and the entire nation of Israel with foreign gods, and it was fitting that he should end his life in company with harlots.

ᴧ First Impressions ᴧ

1. How was Jehoshaphat different from Ahab? Why did Jehoshaphat agree to go into battle with Ahab?

2. What ungodly marriages have we witnessed in these studies? How have such "unequal yokings" affected God's people in these studies?

3. *Why did Ahab surround himself with false prophets? Why did he heed their advice, even when he knew it was wrong? How do people do the same thing today?*

4. *Why did Ahab disguise himself when he went into battle? What did he think he would gain? What did this reveal about his understanding of God's truth?*

◠ Some Key Principles ◠

Speak the truth—especially in the face of opposition.

Ahab hated Micaiah because he always said things that upset the king. When everyone else was predicting success and glory for Ahab, Micaiah would come along and predict doom and gloom. What made it much worse was that Micaiah was always right—because he was speaking God's message rather than his own opinion. It wasn't so much that Ahab hated Micaiah personally; it was more that Ahab hated God's Word.

Micaiah and Elijah had two things in common: they were both hated by Ahab and they both spoke God's truth with boldness—even in the face of opposition. They stood in contrast to the world around them because they spoke the truth to a world that only wanted to hear pleasant words. But what good are pleasant words if they aren't true? Ahab was led to destruction by listening to pleasant words, yet he might have become a godly king had he listened to the truth. Sometimes the truth is not pleasant to hear, but it is always ultimately the most loving thing to tell others. A doctor might bring news of a health problem that upsets us when we hear it, but it is better to act on that truth than to pretend it isn't so. Paul warned Timothy of this very danger: "For the time will come when they will not endure sound doctrine, but according to their own desires, because they have itching ears, they will heap up for themselves teachers; and they will turn their ears away from the truth, and be turned aside to fables" (2 Timothy 4:3–4). Though God's Word may contain things that we find uncomfortable at first, it is a sword that still must be wielded.

What good is it to have a sharp sword during combat, if the soldier refuses to use it? Christians must remember that we are living in a battle zone, and the war for men's souls is raging all around us. As Paul exhorted Timothy, "I charge you therefore before God and the Lord Jesus Christ, who will judge the living and the dead at His appearing and His kingdom: Preach the word! Be ready in season and out of season. Convince, rebuke, exhort, with all longsuffering and teaching" (2 Timothy 4:1–2). Use God's sword with love—but use it!

Test the teachings of men against the truths of Scripture to determine whether their words are from God.

Ahab surrounded himself with hundreds of false prophets, men who could be counted on to say the things that the king wanted to hear. These false prophets made no attempt to ask God for wisdom, yet they spoke authoritatively in God's name, claiming that their words were true. But the Bible gives us a rare glimpse behind the scenes, and we discover that the Lord had actually permitted a lying spirit—the devil himself—to lead these men into speaking lies.

The world is filled with false prophets today, men and women who claim to know truth but who actually speak lies. Many of these people can be very convincing, and their followers may be legion—but this does not make their words true. Christians are called upon to test every teaching and every doctrine against the Scriptures to determine what is true and what is false. Any teacher or prophet or leader who makes any claims that contradict the Bible should be considered a false prophet.

John warned us of this in one of his letters: "Beloved, do not believe every spirit, but test the spirits, whether they are of God; because many false prophets have gone out into the world. By this you know the Spirit of God: Every spirit that confesses that Jesus Christ has come in the flesh is of God, and every spirit that does not confess that Jesus Christ has come in the flesh is not of God. And this is the spirit of the Antichrist, which you have heard was coming, and is now already in the world" (1 John 4:1–3). The Christians at Berea tested everything that Paul taught by comparing his words—daily—against the Scriptures (Acts 17:11). That is the pattern for all Christians: test all teachings against the Bible, and anything that contradicts God's Word is false.

God cannot be fooled.

Despite how tragic it is, the manner of Ahab's death has notes of irony and humor. Ahab was clearly told by Micaiah that he would die in this battle, yet rather than repent and ask God for forgiveness, Ahab tried to manipulate God. Ahab had the prophet jailed, and said that the prophet was not to be released until Ahab returned from battle—as if the Lord would be forced to spare Ahab so that Micaiah could be freed from jail. Then Ahab disguised himself as he went to battle. It appears that Ahab thought God could not kill him if God could not find him. Obviously, the Lord saw through the disguise, and when the archer shot Ahab "at random," his attempt to avoid the judgment for his sin failed. Ahab learned what should have been an obvious lesson: God's judgment cannot be avoided, because God cannot be fooled.

Paul describes this truth in his letter to the Galatians: "Do not be deceived, God is not mocked; for whatever a man sows, this he will also reap" (Galatians 6:7). People often think that somehow they will be able to outwit God and thus avoid judgment for their sins. The reality is that this trickery is impossible, and all sin will be judged. However, God did provide a way to escape the eternal consequences of this judgment. Because He was sinless, when Jesus was crucified it was not for His sins, but for the sins of others. If a person believes that the death of Jesus was payment for his sins, and that God raised Jesus from the grave, that person will be spared the judgment of God. God cannot be tricked or fooled. The only escape from judgment is through belief in the gospel.

Digging Deeper

5. *Why did God send a lying spirit into the false prophets? What does this reveal about God's character? about His sovereignty?*

6. *According to Scripture, what is the test to determine whether a prophet is speaking God's Word? How does this apply to Christians today?*

7. In what ways do people today choose to heed the words of false prophets? Why do people deliberately reject God's truth in favor of such false prophets?

8. When have you boldly spoken the truth, even though it was unpopular? What was the result? When have you not spoken the truth out of fear? What was the result?

⤳ Taking It Personally ⤳

9. Do you test every teaching by comparing it to the Bible? Do you read the Bible on a daily basis? If not, make a plan to begin reading one chapter each day for the coming week.

10. How do you see others try to avoid God's judgment? In your own life, how does the knowledge that Jesus paid the penalty for your sin affect the way you view the judgment of God?

Section 4:

Summary

Notes and Prayer Requests

⟡ 12 ⟡
REVIEWING KEY PRINCIPLES

⟡ LOOKING BACK ⟡

Over the course of the last eleven studies, we have seen the nation of Israel divide into two separate nations, and we have met some of the kings of the northern tribes. In every case, from Solomon onward, those kings refused to obey the Word of God, choosing instead to live as they pleased and worship whatever god they chose. We have also met the prophets of God who confronted those kings, speaking the truth boldly and at great cost to themselves.

One theme has remained constant throughout these studies: *God is faithful*, and those who obey Him will grow in faithfulness as well. The kings of Israel proved themselves to be unfaithful—not only to the nation that they were supposed to be shepherding but to God Himself. In contrast, God's prophets were faithful, both to God and to His people, even though they were in danger of losing life or liberty. When we are faithful to God's Word, we will always discover that He is faithful to us.

Here are a few of the major principles we have found. There are many more that we don't have room to reiterate, so take some time to review the earlier studies—or better still, to meditate upon the passages in Scripture that we have covered. Ask the Holy Spirit to give you wisdom and insight into His Word. He will not refuse.

⟡ SOME KEY PRINCIPLES ⟡

Christians are called to complete obedience, not to partial obedience.

Solomon began his reign well, devoting himself to wisdom and to God's Word. But as time went along, he began to drift away from obedience, making compromises and choosing which of God's commands to obey and which to ignore. One of his first mistakes was to marry "foreign women," women whose hearts were devoted to foreign gods. This caused

Solomon to be unequally yoked, and his many wives (another departure from God's commands) constantly urged him to join them in their pagan religious practices.

God does not give His people the option to customize His Word, choosing for themselves which principles they will incorporate into their lives and which commandments they will ignore. This would be like a soldier telling his commanding officer that he'll obey the officer's commands if and when he gets around to it. Yet this attitude is prevalent in God's church today, as believers attempt to rewrite Scripture to satisfy cultural norms or personal preferences.

The Lord expects His people to live in accordance with the full Word of God, following all of its precepts and living in obedience to all of its commandments. Solomon's life provides a sobering example of what can happen to Christians who pick and choose what parts of Scripture they will apply to their lives, and we will see this same trend in other kings of Israel. The Lord wants His people to take warning from the examples of these kings, devoting our hearts and minds to full obedience instead of following in their wayward footsteps.

Divine sovereignty does not nullify human responsibility.

The Lord prophesied that He would tear the kingdom away from Solomon's son, dividing the nation of Israel into two separate kingdoms. He brought this about, using the foolish decisions of Rehoboam and the rebellious spirit of Israel to accomplish His purpose—yet this did not exonerate the king of Israel from culpability for his foolishness, while the people of Israel were also responsible for their sin. God is indeed sovereign over all the affairs of mankind, but this does not mean that He will not judge individuals for their actions.

Jesus again provides the perfect example of this principle. It was God's plan from the foundation of the world that His perfect Son should offer Himself as a sacrifice to redeem sinful men, and God used the evil deeds of those who rejected Christ to accomplish that plan. Yet this did not exonerate those who crucified Christ; neither does it exonerate anyone who rejects Jesus as the only way to salvation and peace with God.

The good news in this principle is that God uses all things to further His purposes in our lives. When we live in obedience to His Word, we can rest in the assurance that God is completely sovereign over all the events and circumstances that come our way, and He will turn all things to His glory and our blessing. "All things work together for good to those who love God, to those who are the called according to His purpose" (Romans 8:28).

Sin is never trivial.

Jeroboam instituted idolatry in Israel, attempting to mix it together with the nation's worship of God. This was a grievous sin, for which Jeroboam was judged by the Lord, yet Ahab acted "as though it had been a trivial thing" (1 Kings 16:31). By the time Ahab became king, the nation had been embracing Jeroboam's sinful practices for some fifty years, and the people had probably grown so accustomed to it that it seemed normal. This attitude of shrugging off sin led Ahab into even greater wickedness, and eventually brought about the downfall of all Israel.

Sin is never trivial in God's eyes, but when it is ignored or indulged, a believer can become inured. We can grow so accustomed to wickedness that we cease to be bothered by it, even accepting it as normal behavior in the world around us. The danger of this nonchalance is that if we don't take sin seriously, we can begin to slide into embracing it ourselves.

God hates sin, and He calls His people to hate it as He does. It is easy to become complacent about disobedience, and believers must guard against becoming comfortable with sin by spending time in God's Word and in regular fellowship with other believers. As James warns us, "Friendship with the world is enmity with God[.] Whoever therefore wants to be a friend of the world makes himself an enemy of God.... Draw near to God and He will draw near to you. Cleanse your hands, you sinners; and purify your hearts, you double-minded" (James 4:4, 8).

When we disobey God, we sell out our soul to sin.

Ahab wanted Naboth's vineyard; Naboth wouldn't sell. Ahab bartered and pleaded; Naboth stood firm. Ahab pouted; Naboth ignored him. So the mighty king of Israel, who had just won an amazing military victory against a world superpower, stomped off to his bedroom to sulk. He threw himself on his bed, turned his face to the wall, and pettishly refused to eat any food. Ahab threw a temper tantrum, but when Elijah confronted him, notice how Elijah described Ahab's sin: "You have sold yourself to do evil" (1 Kings 21:20).

Ahab had murdered in exchange for a vineyard. In 1 Kings 20, he had ignored the Lord's command in exchange for a bribe. The Lord describes both of these sins as a form of selling out. Ahab had a choice: obey God, or forfeit his loyalty to fulfill his sinful desires. He wanted a vineyard, so he allowed his wife to murder an innocent man.

When a person sins, he is saying that there is something he desires more than obedience to God. He is saying that a certain pleasure, or in this case a vineyard, will bring more joy than the joy that comes from obedience. Sin is the selling out of our soul. It has been said that every man has a price; in Ahab's case, he sold out for a vineyard. He desired sin, and he sold himself to serve it. This is what it means to be a slave to sin. When a person sells his loyalty in exchange for sin, he becomes a servant to sin, and an enemy to God.

Whatever the Lord gives you to do, do it with all your might.

Obadiah had risen to a great height in his career. The king's steward held a position of tremendous trust and authority, as the king generally gave him full responsibility over his entire household. Indeed, the king trusted his very life to his steward, since one of the steward's responsibilities was to ensure that nobody poisoned the king's food. Obadiah had no doubt attained this position, from a human perspective, by virtue of diligent and skillful work. Whatever Obadiah did, he did it well.

But there is another side to this situation that must not be overlooked. The truth is that Obadiah had been placed in this important position by the Lord, and at least part of God's reason for placing him there was so that he could save the lives of the prophets during Jezebel's murderous spree. And here again Obadiah's diligent habits came into play: he saw an opportunity to serve the Lord, and he took full advantage of it. You might say that Obadiah was given the work of saving lives, and he saved those lives with all his might.

Obadiah was a servant to a king, and he ensured that his work was fit for a king. Christians should cultivate this same attitude, for we are servants to the King of kings. Whatever we are called to do, even the most mundane responsibilities, we should strive to make our work fit for the King. "Whatever you do," Paul wrote, "do it heartily, as to the Lord and not to men, knowing that from the Lord you will receive the reward of the inheritance; for you serve the Lord Christ" (Colossians 3:23–24).

Be courageous.

Obadiah lived in a very difficult situation. He was loyal to the king, and his position as steward required that he carry out the king's will in all things. The problem was that Jezebel hated the people of God and made it her priority to destroy the Lord's prophets at every opportunity. Obadiah's first loyalty was to the Lord, and he could not comply with the queen's wishes; in fact, he was compelled to fight against her determination to murder the prophets.

So Obadiah took a terrible risk by hiding one hundred prophets in caves, protecting them from Jezebel's murderous hatred. Had he been caught, the queen would have put him to death without hesitation, and the king would have viewed his actions as open treachery. His bravery on that occasion called for secrecy, but the Lord next called him to act courageously and openly on His behalf. If Obadiah had given in to his fears, he might have refused to obey God openly, and that would have been like a public denial of the Lord. He would in effect have been saying that he feared the king's wrath more than he trusted God's sovereignty.

Fear causes us to distrust God's loving hand of provision and protection. It grows when we focus on the thing that frightens us, rather than on the God who protects us. This is the reason that the Lord commands His people to be courageous, because faith requires courage—believing that God will protect His people, and acting on that belief. The Lord's words to Joshua apply to us as well: "Have I not commanded you? Be strong and of good courage; do not be afraid, nor be dismayed, for the LORD your God is with you wherever you go" (Joshua 1:9).

Syncretism is a form of idolatry.

Syncretism refers to the act of mixing together elements from different religions to create a sort of hybrid religious system. The process can refer to intermingling diverse religious practices, or it can refer to those who attempt to reconcile opposing viewpoints. Jeroboam committed the sin of syncretism when he attempted to mingle pagan idolatry together with God's commanded worship. It is easy to see the idolatry of Jeroboam's acts, since he literally created two golden calves for the people to worship.

But syncretism is still idolatry even when it doesn't involve golden calves. The basic motivation behind syncretism is rebellion against God's Word. A person decides that he wants to worship God in his own way, and rejects certain aspects of Scripture in favor of his own ideas or practices. This is the idolatry of self, making oneself to be equal with God and pushing God into the background, just as Jeroboam did. The world continually encourages syncretism for the simple reason that it hates the teachings of Christ and does everything in its power to move believers away from God's Word. The claim that the gospel must be made "relevant" to our culture is used as an excuse by many to ignore some scriptural principles and add in principles that are not scriptural—but such attempts are syncretistic, attempting to mix the teachings of the world into the doctrines of God's Word.

The Bible is the final authority on how to approach God, and no man has the privilege of rewriting Scripture to fit his own desires or to fit into the culture of the world around him. When cultural teachings and practices go against the teachings of the Bible, then we are called to choose between the two—but not to attempt some compromise incorporating elements of both. Elijah confronted the people of Israel at Mount Carmel on this very issue, calling them to choose once and for all to serve God, and to serve Him in His way, not their own way. Anything else is idolatry.

Test the teachings of men against the truths of Scripture to determine whether their words are from God.

Ahab surrounded himself with hundreds of false prophets, men who could be counted on to say the things that the king wanted to hear. These false prophets made no attempt to ask God for wisdom, yet they spoke authoritatively in God's name, claiming that their words were true. But the Bible gives us a rare glimpse behind the scenes, and we discover that the Lord had actually permitted a lying spirit—the devil himself—to lead these men into speaking lies.

The world is filled with false prophets today, men and women who claim to know truth but who actually speak lies. Many of these people can be very convincing, and their followers may be legion—but this does not make their words true. Christians are called upon to test every teaching and every doctrine against the Scriptures to determine what is true and what is false. Any teacher or prophet or leader who makes any claims that contradict the Bible should be considered a false prophet.

John warned us of this in one of his letters: "Beloved, do not believe every spirit, but test the spirits, whether they are of God; because many false prophets have gone out into the world. By this you know the Spirit of God: Every spirit that confesses that Jesus Christ has come in the flesh is of God, and every spirit that does not confess that Jesus Christ has come in the flesh is not of God. And this is the spirit of the Antichrist, which you have heard was coming, and is now already in the world" (1 John 4:1–3). The Christians at Berea tested everything that Paul taught by comparing his words—daily—against the Scriptures (Acts 17:11). That is the pattern for all Christians: test all teachings against the Bible, and anything that contradicts God's Word is false.

↜ Digging Deeper ↝

1. *What are some of the more important things you have learned from 1 Kings?*

2. Which of the concepts or principles have you found most encouraging? Which have been most challenging?

3. What aspects of "walking with God" are you already doing in your life? Which areas need strengthening?

4. Which of the characters we've studied have you felt the most drawn to? How might you emulate that person in your own life?

↳ TAKING IT PERSONALLY ↲

5. Have you taken a definite stand for Jesus Christ? Have you accepted His free gift of salvation? If not, what is preventing you?

6. What areas of your personal life have you been most convicted in during this study? What exact things will you do to address these convictions? Be specific.

7. What have you learned about the character of God during this study? How has this insight affected your worship or prayer life?

8. List below the specific things you want to see God do in your life in the coming month. List also the things that you intend to change in your own life in that time. Return to this list in one month, and hold yourself accountable to fulfill these things.

If you would like to continue in your study of the Old Testament, read the next title in this series, *Losing the Promised Land*, or the previous title, *End of an Era*.